WHY WE BELIEVE THE BIBLE

WHY WE BELIEVE
THE BIBLE

STUDY GUIDE DEVELOPED BY DESIRING GOD

CROSSWAY BOOKS
WHEATON, ILLINOIS

Why We Believe the Bible Study Guide

Published by Crossway Books
a publishing ministry of Good News Publishers
1300 Crescent Street
Wheaton, Illinois 60187

This study guide is based on and is a companion to *Why We Believe the Bible* (DVD) by John Piper (Crossway Books, 2009).

Cover design: Amy Bristow

Cover photo: iStock

First printing 2009

Printed in the United States of America

Trade paperback ISBN: 978-1-4335-0771-7

PDF ISBN: 978-1-4335-0772-4

Mobipocket ISBN: 978-1-4335-0773-1

VP 18 17 16 15 14 13 12 11 10 09
14 13 12 11 10 9 8 7 6 5 4 3 2 1

CONTENTS

INTRODUCTION TO THIS STUDY GUIDE

JESUS SAID SOME VERY HARD THINGS. So hard, in fact, that many who followed him turned back and wanted nothing to do with him. On one such occasion, Jesus turned to the twelve disciples and asked, "Do you want to go away as well?" John records Simon Peter's answer: "Lord, to whom shall we go? You have the words of eternal life, and we have believed, and have come to know, that you are the Holy One of God" (John 6:67–69). Simon Peter knew that no one spoke like Jesus. Jesus spoke with authority. He spoke words of eternal life and Peter believed.

The situation is similar today when we come to the Bible. For many, the Bible is either offensive or irrelevant: a patchwork quilt of antiquated dogma, conflicting data, and unfounded myths. It may have value as a historical relic, or perhaps we may glean some insight from its ethical teachings, but it is certainly not reliable as a guide to all of life. Furthermore, other religious texts such as the Qur'an, the Bhagavad Gita, the Book of Mormon, and the Buddhist Sutras grapple for our allegiance. We are a torn people in need of clarity.

The purpose of this study guide is to help you part the philosophical fog and delight in the cast-iron reliability of the Word of God. Paul had similar desires for Timothy when he wrote, "All Scripture is breathed out by God and profitable for teaching, for reproof, for correction, and for training in righteousness" (2 Timothy 3:16). Our prayer is that you would feel the life-giving nature of these words and say of the Scriptures, "More to be desired are they than gold, even much fine gold; sweeter also than honey and drippings from the honeycomb" (Psalm 19:10).

After all, the stakes are high. Paul said all Scripture is breathed out by God. Peter said Jesus had the words of eternal life. If they are right, then to reject the Scriptures is not simply being misinformed. It is suicidal. May God be pleased to use this resource to protect thousands from stopping their ears to his voice and to cause them to heed the words of Isaiah: "Listen diligently to me, and eat what is good, and delight yourselves in rich food. Incline your ear, and come to me; hear, that your soul may live" (Isaiah 55:2–3).

This study guide is designed to be used in a twelve-session,[1] guided group study that focuses on the *Why We Believe the Bible* DVD set.[2] After an introductory lesson, each subsequent lesson examines one 30-minute session[3] from the DVD. You, the learner, are encouraged to prepare for the viewing of each session by reading and reflecting upon Scripture, by considering key quotations, and by asking yourself penetrating questions. Your preparatory work for each lesson is marked with the heading "Before You Watch the DVD, Study and Prepare" in Lessons 2–11.

The workload is conveniently divided into five daily (and manageable) assignments. There is also a section suggesting further study. This work is to be completed individually before the group convenes to view the DVD and discuss the material.

> Throughout this study guide, paragraphs printed in a shaded box (like this one) are excerpts from a book written by John Piper or from the Desiring God Web site, or excerpts from other sources. They are included to supplement the study questions and to summarize key or provocative points.

The second section in Lessons 2–11, entitled "Further Up and Further In," is designed for the learner who wants to explore the concepts and ideas introduced in the lesson in greater detail. This section is not required, but will deepen your understanding of the material. This section requires that you read online sermons or articles from the Desiring God Web site (www.desiringGod.org) and answer relevant questions. These sermons can be found by performing a Title Search at the Desiring God Web site.

The third section in Lessons 2–11, entitled "While You Watch the DVD, Take Notes," is to be completed as the DVD is playing. This section includes fill-in-the-blanks and leaves space for note-taking. You are encouraged to engage with the DVD by filling in the appropriate blanks and writing down other notes that will aid you in the group discussion.

The fourth section in each normal lesson is "After You Watch the DVD, Discuss What You've Learned." Three discussion questions are provided to guide and focus the conversation. You may record, in the spaces provided, notes that will help you contribute to the conversation. Or, you may use this space to record things from the discussion that you want to remember.

The fifth and final section is an application section: "After You Discuss, Make Application." You will be challenged to record a "take-away point" and to engage in a certain activity that is a fitting response to the content presented in the lesson.

Group leaders will want to find the Leader's Guide, included at the end of this study guide, immediately.

Life transformation will only occur by the grace of God. Therefore, we highly encourage you to seek the Lord in prayer throughout the learning process. Pray that God would open your eyes to see wonderful things in his Word. Pray that he would grant you the insight and concentration you need in order to get the most from this resource. Pray that God would cause you not merely to understand the truth, but also to rejoice in it. And pray that the discussion in your group would be mutually encouraging and edifying. We've included objectives at the beginning of each lesson. These objectives won't be realized without the gracious work of God through prayer.

NOTES

1. While this study guide is ideally suited for a twelve-session study, it is possible to complete it in six sessions. For instructions on how to use this study guide for a six-session group study, turn to Appendix A: Six-Session Intensive Option.
2. Although this resource is designed to be used in a group setting, it can also be used by the independent learner. Such a learner would have to decide how to use this resource in the most beneficial way. We would suggest doing everything but the group discussion, if possible.
3. Thirty minutes is only an approximation. Some sessions are longer; others are shorter.

LESSON 1

INTRODUCTION TO *WHY WE BELIEVE THE BIBLE*

LESSON OBJECTIVES

It is our prayer that after you have finished this lesson . . .

- You will have a better sense of how you and others in your group approach the Bible.
- Your curiosity will be roused, and questions will come to mind.
- You will be eager to better cherish and defend the reliability of the Scriptures.

ABOUT YOURSELF

1) What is your name?

2) Tell the group something about yourself that they probably don't already know.

3) What are you hoping to learn from this study?

A PREVIEW OF *WHY WE BELIEVE THE BIBLE*

1) Think about your own history in relation to the Bible. How have you changed in the way you view the Scriptures? What were some influences that brought you to where you are today?

2) List some common objections to the believability of the Scriptures. Circle one that you feel is most widespread today. How would you respond to this objection?

LESSON 2

WHY DOES IT MATTER IF THE BIBLE IS TRUE? (PART 1)

A Companion Study to the Why We Believe the Bible DVD, Session 1

LESSON OBJECTIVES

It is our prayer that after you have finished this lesson . . .

- You will feel the importance of believing that the Bible is reliable.
- You will better grasp the life-giving purpose of the Word of God.
- You will be more aware of the opposition that exists against the trustworthiness of Scripture.

BEFORE YOU WATCH THE DVD, STUDY AND PREPARE

DAY 1: WHAT'S AT STAKE?

Before examining the case for believing the Scriptures, it is important to ask why the question matters in the first place.

***QUESTION 1:** Suppose someone were to ask you, "Why does it matter whether the Bible is true?" How would you answer him? Out of the possible responses you could give, try to identify the one you feel is the most compelling. Provide any scriptural support you can think of.[1]

Now consider the importance of the question through Peter's eyes as he addresses the difficulty of some of Paul's sayings.

2 PETER 3:15–16

> 15 *And count the patience of our Lord as salvation, just as our*
> *beloved brother Paul also wrote to you according to the wisdom*
> *given him,* 16 *as he does in all his letters when he speaks in them of these matters. There are some things in them that are hard to understand, which the ignorant and unstable twist to their own destruction, as they do the other Scriptures.*

QUESTION 2: According to Peter, what is the danger of neglecting the true meaning of Scripture? Underline the phrase that explicitly identifies the consequence. What type of destruction does Peter have in mind? See 2 Peter 3:7 for further help.

DAY 2: SWEETER THAN HONEY

Examine the portrayal of the Scriptures in the following passage.

PSALM 19:7–10

7 The law of the LORD is perfect, reviving the soul; the testimony
of the LORD is sure, making wise the simple; 8 the precepts of
the LORD are right, rejoicing the heart; the commandment of
the LORD is pure, enlightening the eyes; 9 the fear of the LORD
is clean, enduring forever; the rules of the LORD are true, and
righteous altogether. 10 More to be desired are they than gold,
even much fine gold; sweeter also than honey and drippings of
the honeycomb.

***QUESTION 3:** David uses words such as "law," "testimony," and "precepts" to refer to the words of the Lord. Underline each word or phrase that explains what the Scriptures are like. What does their united testimony say about the Bible? How should that affect the way we feel about the Bible today?

Reflect on the testimony of a man named "Little Bilney" who was an English Reformer born in 1495. Notice the connection in his story between salvation and treasuring the words of the Bible.

> I chanced upon this sentence of St. Paul (O most sweet and comfortable sentence to my soul!) in 1 Timothy 1: "It is a true saying, and worthy of all men to be embraced, that Christ Jesus came into the world to save sinners; of whom

> I am the chief and principal." This one sentence, through God's instruction and inward working, which I did not then perceive, did so exhilarate my heart, being before wounded with the guilt of my sins, and being almost in despair, that . . . immediately I . . . felt a marvelous comfort and quietness, in so much that "my bruised bones leaped for joy." After this, the Scriptures began to be more pleasant to me than the honey or the honeycomb.[2]

QUESTION 4: According to Little Bilney's account, how does a person come to experience the words of the Bible as "more pleasant . . . than the honey or the honeycomb"? What must take place before this can be truly felt?

DAY 3: HIS DELIGHT IS IN THE LAW OF THE LORD

Psalm 1 offers a vivid picture of what the righteous man looks like. Read this passage and then answer the following question.

PSALM 1

> 1 *Blessed is the man who walks not in the counsel of the wicked, nor stands in the way of sinners, nor sits in the seat of scoffers;* 2 *but his delight is in the law of the* LORD*, and on his law he meditates day and night.* 3 *He is like a tree planted by streams of water that yields its fruit in its season, and its leaf does not wither. In all that he does, he prospers.* 4 *The wicked are not so, but are like chaff that the wind drives away.* 5 *Therefore the wicked will not stand in the judgment, nor sinners in the con-*

> *gregation of the righteous;* [6] *for the* Lord *knows the way of the righteous, but the way of the wicked will perish.*

QUESTION 5: Draw a line down the center of your answer space. In the left column, list the descriptions of the wicked. What do they do? What are they like? What is their destiny? Now list the descriptions of the righteous man in the right column and answer the same questions. What is the distinguishing mark of the righteous man? To whose words does he listen? What type of listening does the Psalmist have in mind?

What exactly is it about the Bible that protects a person from destruction and provides him with streams that nourish his roots? It is possible to answer this question wrongly. Observe the way Jesus rebukes the Pharisees in the following passage.

JOHN 5:39–40

> [39] *You search the Scriptures because you think that in them you have eternal life; and it is they that bear witness about me,* [40] *yet you refuse to come to me that you may have life.*

***QUESTION 6:** What was wrong with the way the Pharisees approached the Bible? How does Jesus correct them? According to this, what exactly is the relationship between the Scriptures and eternal life?

> The Lord opens the eyes of the heart to see the glory of Christ in the Word. God has chosen in this age to reveal himself to the world mainly through the incarnate Word, Jesus Christ, by means of the written Word, the Bible.[3]

DAY 4: A LONG LINE OF LOVERS

One of the gifts God has given to his church is a heritage of corporate statements that detail what it means for the Bible to be reliable. One such statement is the Chicago Statement on Biblical Inerrancy, written in 1978. Below is an excerpt from this statement.

> 2. Holy Scripture, being God's own Word, written by men prepared and superintended by His Spirit, is of infallible divine authority in all matters upon which it touches: It is to be believed, as God's instruction, in all that it affirms; obeyed, as God's command, in all that it requires; embraced, as God's pledge, in all that it promises. . . . 4. Being wholly and verbally God-given, Scripture is without error or fault in all its teaching, no less in what it states about God's acts in creation, about the events of world history, and about its own literary origins under God, than in its witness to God's saving grace in individual lives.

QUESTION 7: In the space below, list several key words the Chicago Statement provides to describe what it means for the Bible to be trustworthy. In what areas is the Bible without error?

Now examine the Chicago Statement in light of the following passage.

2 TIMOTHY 3:16

> [16] *All Scripture is breathed out by God and profitable for teaching, for reproof, for correction, and for training in righteousness.*

***QUESTION 8:** What is the significance of the phrase "breathed out by God"? Why does it matter that this quality applies to "all Scripture"? What does this imply for those who reject all or part of the Bible?

DAY 5: THE BIBLE UNDER FIRE

Not everyone agrees that all of the Bible can be trusted. Interact with the following portion of a letter submitted to the *Minneapolis Star-Tribune* by the Minnesota Atheists (published October 17, 1992).

> One of the few worthwhile statements in the Bible is, "You shall know the truth and the truth shall make you free." . . . Knowledge of the Bible is hindered by the informal censorship imposed by religious leaders who would rather their followers didn't know what's in it—the innumerable contradictions, historical errors, plagiarism, absurdities, meaningless prophecies, myths presented as historical fact, and

countless instances of divinely ordered or approved atrocities. . . . It is true that the Bible has some worthwhile material, including entertaining stories, inspirational sentiments and astute observations about human behavior. However, these worthwhile parts could probably be contained in a pamphlet.[5]

***QUESTION 9:** Summarize the argument of these authors in one sentence. How would you respond to someone who held these convictions about the Bible?

The letter quotes Jesus' words in John 8:32, "And you will know the truth and the truth will set you free." Study this verse in its original context to discern what Jesus meant when he said this.

JOHN 8:31–38

[31] So Jesus said to the Jews who had believed in him, "If you abide
in my word, you are truly my disciples, [32] and you will know the
truth, and the truth will set you free." [33] They answered him,
"We are offspring of Abraham and have never been enslaved
to anyone. How is it that you say, ëYou will become free'?"
[34] Jesus answered them, "Truly, truly, I say to you, everyone who
commits sin is a slave to sin. [35] The slave does not remain in the
house forever; the son remains forever. [36] So if the Son sets you
free, you will be free indeed. [37] I know that you are offspring
of Abraham; yet you seek to kill me because my word finds no
place in you. [38] I speak of what I have seen with my Father, and
you do what you have heard from your father."

QUESTION 10: What is the truth Jesus is referring to in John 8:32? How does a person know this truth? What is the slavery from which this truth will set a person free? Why did the Jews want to kill Jesus?

FURTHER UP AND FURTHER IN

Note: The "Further Up and Further In" section is for those who want to study more. It is a section for further reference and going deeper. The phrase "further up and further in" is borrowed from C. S. Lewis.

As noted in the Introduction, each lesson in this study guide provides the opportunity for you to do further study. In this section, you will have the opportunity to read a sermon or an article and answer some questions about what you read.

Read or listen to "Contend for the Faith," an online sermon at the Desiring God Web site.

QUESTION 11: According to John Piper, which verse in Jude contains the main point of the book? Write out this verse in the space below.

QUESTION 12: Why do such books as the Qur'an and the Book of Mormon contradict Jude's teaching that the faith has been "once for all delivered to the saints" (Jude 3)?

John Piper refers to Jude 22–23. Read this passage and then answer the following question.

JUDE 22–23

> [22] *And have mercy on those who doubt;* [23] *save others by snatching them out of the fire; to others show mercy with fear, hating even the garment stained by the flesh.*

QUESTION 13: According to John Piper, what two things are involved in contending for the faith from these two verses? How does this affect the way we think about contending for the reliability of the Scriptures?

Read Section 1 of the Bethlehem Baptist Church (BBC) Elder Affirmation of Faith entitled "Scripture, the Word of God Written."[6]

QUESTION 14: List the factors that can inhibit a person's understanding of biblical texts. Have any of these been true in your own life? Explain.

Study the following passage.

1 CORINTHIANS 2:12–14

> [12] *Now we have received not the spirit of the world, but the Spirit who is from God, that we might understand the things freely given us by God.* [13] *And we impart this in words not taught by human wisdom but taught by the Spirit, interpreting spiritual truths to those who are spiritual.* [14] *The natural person does not accept the things of the Spirit of God, for they are folly to him, and he is not able to understand them because they are spiritually discerned.*

QUESTION 15: According to this passage, what is the ultimate reason behind a person's refusal to accept the authority and trustworthiness of the Bible? How should we respond in light of this? Be specific.

WHILE YOU WATCH THE DVD, TAKE NOTES

What is the first reason John Piper gives for why he is taking up the topic of the Bible's reliability?

need to be able to give an answer for the hope that we have

According to John Piper, what was the greatest thing to come out of the 1974 Lausanne Conference?

Its affirmation of faith - strong statement on inspiration + inerrancy of the Bible

If two people are in an argument and absolute truth is not functioning as an arbiter between them, what is the only thing left to appeal to?

epistimology?

power - "might will make right" = def. of a tyrant

What two centuries does John Piper say we ought to know?

1st + 20th centuries

Christ - introduced the best

tyrants like Hitler, Mussolini, etc. = the worst

→ There is such a thing as truth + the Bible contains it.

"It would be truer to say that the Qur'an is for Muslims what Christ is for Christians."

AFTER YOU WATCH THE DVD, DISCUSS WHAT YOU'VE LEARNED

1) Why is it necessary to anchor our understanding of the Bible in the observable meaning of its words rather than in subjective impressions that come from outside the Bible?

Because subjective impressions aren't necessarily inspired by God but the Bible's words are.

2) John Piper quoted Michael Novak, who said that those who reject absolute truth "prepare the jails of the twenty-first century. They do the work of tyrants." Do you agree? Why is it important to defend the existence of absolute truth?

That makes sense, and I already do see it happening. Because without an absolute truth, everyone will just do what's right in their own eyes with no repercussions. There wouldn't be a clear right or wrong.

3) Discuss the difference between the Qur'an and the Bible as it was presented in this lesson. What are some implications of the fact that the Bible is "infinitely translatable"?

Qur'an = dropped from heaven by God supposedly

Bible = the account of Jesus who came down from heaven.

4 being infinitely translatable means that it's potentially accessible to everyone, not exclusive to readers of one language

AFTER YOU DISCUSS, MAKE APPLICATION

1) What was the most meaningful part of this lesson for you? Was there a sentence, a concept, or an idea that really struck you? Why? Record your thoughts in the space below.

2) Pray through Psalm 19:7–11 this week. Thank God for the characteristics of his Word that David describes and ask him to help you feel this way about the Bible more and more. Record your reflections below.

NOTES

1. Questions marked with an asterisk (*) are questions that we deem to be particularly significant. If your group is completing this study using the six-session intensive option, we recommend that you complete these questions first and then, if time permits, complete the remaining questions. For more information, see Appendix A—Six-Session Intensive Option.

2. Quoted by John Piper in *Desiring God* (Sisters, OR: Multnomah, 2003), 146.

3. John Piper, *When I Don't Desire God* (Wheaton, IL: Crossway, 2004), 96.

4. Excerpt taken from an online resource at the Desiring God Web site entitled, "Why We Believe the Bible, Part 1." Throughout this

study guide, articles and sermons at the Desiring God Web site (www.desiringGod.org) may be found by performing a Title Search on the home page.

5. John Piper, "Why We Believe the Bible, Part 1," an online resource at the Desiring God Web site.
6. This document is accessible at http://hopeingod.org/resources/images/1230.pdf.

LESSON 3

WHY DOES IT MATTER IF THE BIBLE IS TRUE? (PART 2)

A Companion Study to the Why We Believe the Bible DVD, Session 2

LESSON OBJECTIVES

It is our prayer that after you have finished this lesson . . .

- You will have an even deeper sense of the importance of believing that the Bible is reliable.
- You will yearn to embrace a life of sacrificial service because of the hope of the resurrection.
- You will be better equipped to handle apparent contradictions in Scripture.

BEFORE YOU WATCH THE DVD, STUDY AND PREPARE

DAY 1: THE GODS OF THE PEOPLES ARE WORTHLESS IDOLS

In the last lesson, you examined some reasons for why it matters whether the Bible is true. In this lesson you will explore further reasons, one of which is the fact that the Scriptures make some astounding claims. If they are true, then the Bible alone has the message of eternal life. To see this, study Psalm 96:5 together with Psalm 115:4–8.

PSALM 96:5

> [5] *For all the gods of the peoples are worthless idols, but the* LORD *made the heavens.*

PSALM 115:4–8

> [4] *Their idols are silver and gold, the work of human hands.*
> [5] *They have mouths, but do not speak; eyes, but do not see.*
> [6] *They have ears, but do not hear; noses, but do not smell.*
> [7] *They have hands, but do not feel; feet, but do not walk; and*
> *they do not make a sound in their throat.* [8] *Those who make*
> *them become like them; so do all who trust in them.*

QUESTION 1: What is the fundamental difference between the Lord and the gods of the peoples? Why does the Psalmist refer to other gods as "worthless idols"? What is the danger of trusting in such idols?

Now consider the universal claim of the following passage.

ISAIAH 45:22–23

> [22] *Turn to me and be saved, all the ends of the earth! For I am God, and there is no other.* [23] *By myself I have sworn; from my mouth has gone out in righteousness a word that shall not return: "To me every knee shall bow, every tongue shall swear allegiance."*

***QUESTION 2:** Meditate on the phrase, "There is no other." What are some implications of the fact that the God who has revealed himself in the Bible is the one true God? From whom does God deserve worship?

DAY 2: JESUS IS THE ONLY WAY TO THE FATHER

Examine John 8:42; John 14:6–7; Acts 4:12; and 1 John 5:12 to see what it looks like to worship the one true God.

JOHN 8:42

> [42] *Jesus said to them, "If God were your Father, you would love me, for I came from God and I am here. I came not of my own accord, but he sent me."*

JOHN 14:6–7

> [6] *Jesus said to him, "I am the way, and the truth, and the life. No one comes to the Father except through me.* [7] *If you had known me, you would have known my Father also. From now on you do know him and have seen him."*

ACTS 4:12

> [12] *And there is salvation in no one else, for there is no other name under heaven given among men by which we must be saved."*

1 JOHN 5:12

> [12] *Whoever has the Son has life; whoever does not have the Son of God does not have life.*

***QUESTION 3:** According to these texts, what is the only way a person can truly worship God and have eternal life? If the Bible is true, what does this say about other religions that reject Jesus, even if they claim to worship God?

> . . . Jesus is so fully God-reflecting and God-exalting that denying him means denying God. Jesus knows that his adversaries "do not have the love of God within [them]" because they do not receive him. "The one who rejects me rejects him who sent me" (Luke 10:16). If they loved God,

they would love him. He makes God known more clearly and more fully than any other revelation. Therefore, it cannot be that one has love for God but rejects Jesus.[1]

Yesterday you examined Isaiah 45:22–23. Refer back to this text after you read the following passage.

PHILIPPIANS 2:8–11

[8] And being found in human form, he humbled himself by
becoming obedient to the point of death, even death on a cross.
[9] Therefore God has highly exalted him and bestowed on him
the name that is above every name, [10] so that at the name of
Jesus every knee should bow, in heaven and on earth and under
the earth, [11] and every tongue confess that Jesus Christ is Lord,
to the glory of God the Father.

QUESTION 4: Underline the phrase from this passage that is a reference to Isaiah 45:23. In Isaiah 45:23, who is speaking? To whom does the apostle Paul apply this statement in Philippians 2:8–11? How does this affect our understanding of Jesus and the seriousness of rejecting him?

DAY 3: A LIFE TO BE PITIED

Another reason why it matters whether the Bible is true is that it would be foolish to live a life of sacrificial service if what God said in the Bible were false.

QUESTION 5: In the space below, list some sacrifices that either you or someone you know have made because of following Jesus. These can be anything from minor frustrations to heart-wrenching losses. Why is this list wasted if the Bible is not trustworthy?

Richard Wurmbrand was a Romanian pastor who served fourteen years in Communist prisons for the sake of the gospel. John Piper responds to a story Wurmbrand told about a Cistercian abbot who defended a life of sacrifice.

> One of the stories he tells is about a Cistercian abbot who was interviewed on Italian television. The interviewer was especially interested in the Cistercian tradition of living in silence and solitude. So he asked the abbot, "And what if you were to realize at the end of your life that atheism is true—that there is no God? Tell me, what if that were true?"
>
> The abbot replied, "Holiness, silence, and sacrifice are beautiful in themselves, even without promise of reward. I still will have used my life well."
>
> Few glimpses into the meaning of life have had a greater impact on my contemplations about suffering. The first impact of the abbot's response was a superficial, romantic surge of glory. But then something stuck. It did not sit well.

Something was wrong. At first I could not figure it out. Then I turned to the great Christian sufferer, the apostle Paul, and was stunned by the gulf between him and the abbot.

Paul's answer to the interviewer's question was utterly contrary to the abbot's answer. The interviewer had asked, "What if your way of life turns out to be a falsehood, and there is no God?" The abbot's answer in essence was, "It was a good and noble life anyway." Paul gave his answer in 1 Corinthians 15:19: "If in this life only we have hoped in Christ, we are of all people most to be pitied." This is the exact opposite of the abbot's answer.[2]

Now evaluate John Piper's response in light of the following passage.

1 CORINTHIANS 15:16–19

16 For if the dead are not raised, not even Christ has been raised.
17 And if Christ has not been raised, your faith is futile and you
are still in your sins. 18 Then those also who have fallen asleep
in Christ have perished. 19 If in Christ we have hope in this life
only, we are of all people most to be pitied.

***QUESTION 6:** After reading this passage, do you agree that the abbot was wrong? Why are we most to be pitied if we only have hope in Christ in this life? What exactly is the hope that justifies a life of sacrificial service? How is this threatened if the Bible is not true?

> So Paul concludes from his hourly danger and his daily dying and his fighting with beasts that the life he has chosen in following Jesus is foolish and pitiable if he will not be raised from the dead. "If in Christ we have hope in this life only, we are of all people most to be pitied." In other words, only the resurrection with Christ and the joys of eternity can make sense out of this suffering.[3]

DAY 4: THE ONLY COMPLETELY TRUE BOOK

Read the following testimony from John Piper.

> The Bible tethers us to reality. We are not free to think and speak whatever might enter our minds or what might be pleasing to any given audience—except God.
>
> By personal calling and Scripture, I am bound to the Word of God and to the preaching of what the Bible says. There are few things that burden me more or refresh me more than saying what I see in the Bible. I love to see what God says in the Bible. I love to savor it. And I love to say it.
>
> I believe with all my heart that this is the way God has appointed for me not to waste my life. His Word is true. The Bible is the only completely true book in the world. It is inspired by God. Rightly understood and followed, it will lead us to everlasting joy with him. There is no greater book or greater truth.[5]

QUESTION 7: Analyze the statement, "The Bible is the only completely true book in the world." Why does it matter that the Bible is *completely* true? What guarantees its truthfulness? How does the fact that the Bible is the *only* completely true book in the world affect the way we think of other books? Can there be any truth in them? Explain.

Meditate on the following passage.

PSALM 12:6

> [6] *The words of the LORD are pure words, like silver refined in a furnace on the ground, purified seven times.*

***QUESTION 8:** To what substance does David compare the words of God? What does the fact that this substance is purified seven times tell us about Scripture? Can there be any impurities or errors in it?

DAY 5: WHAT ABOUT TEXTS THAT SEEM TO DISAGREE?

Many would claim that the Bible is riddled with contradiction. However, if the Bible is completely true, then this alters the way we approach texts that appear contradictory. Consider 1 Samuel 15:11 and 1 Samuel 15:28–29 as an example.

1 SAMUEL 15:11

> [11] *"I regret that I have made Saul king, for he has turned back from following me and has not performed my commandments." And Samuel was angry, and he cried to the LORD all night.*

1 SAMUEL 15:28–29

> [28] *And Samuel said to him, "The LORD has torn the kingdom of Israel from you this day and has given it to a neighbor of yours, who is better than you.* [29] *And also the Glory of Israel will not lie or have regret, for he is not a man, that he should have regret."*

***QUESTION 9:** How can it be that God regrets making Saul king in verse 11 and then claims that he does not have regret in verse 29? Is it possible to understand these verses in a way that maintains the truthfulness of Scripture?

QUESTION 10: List other passages that seem to be saying conflicting things. Choose one set of texts from your list and briefly suggest how they might be reconciled with one another.

FURTHER UP AND FURTHER IN

Another pair of texts that may be challenging to reconcile are James 2:24 and Romans 3:28. Examine each in their broader context.

JAMES 2:20–26

> [20] *Do you want to be shown, you foolish person, that faith apart from works is useless?* [21] *Was not Abraham our father justified by works when he offered up his son Isaac on the altar?* [22] *You see that faith was active along with his works, and faith was completed by his works;* [23] *and the Scripture was fulfilled that says, "Abraham believed God, and it was counted to him as righteousness"—and he was called a friend of God.* [24] *You see that a person is justified by works and not by faith alone.* [25] *And in the same way was not also Rahab the prostitute justified by works when she received the messengers and sent them out by another way?* [26] *For as the body apart from the spirit is dead, so also faith apart from works is dead.*

ROMANS 3:27–31

> [27] *Then what becomes of our boasting? It is excluded. By what kind of law? By a law of works? No, but by the law of faith.* [28] *For we hold that one is justified by faith apart from works of the law.* [29] *Or is God the God of Jews only? Is he not the God of Gentiles also? Yes, of Gentiles also,* [30] *since God is one—who will justify the circumcised by faith and the uncircumcised through faith.* [31] *Do we then overthrow the law by this faith? By no means! On the contrary, we uphold the law.*

QUESTION 11: What does James mean when he says that a person is "justified by works and not by faith alone"? What analogy does he provide to demonstrate his point (verse 26)?

QUESTION 12: What does Paul mean when he says that a person is "justified by faith apart from works of the law"? How do you think he understands works, especially in light of his mention of "boasting"?

QUESTION 13: Given your previous answers, how might James and Paul harmonize with one another?

Now that you have wrestled with the issue personally, interact with John Piper's treatment of these texts.

Read "Does James Contradict Paul?" an online article at the Desiring God Web site.

QUESTION 14: According to John Piper, what is the key question to ask in addressing the tension between James and Paul in this instance?

QUESTION 15: What is the crucial text for seeing Paul and James in harmony with one another? What do Paul and James each mean by the phrase "justification by works"? How does this help us see the agreement between the two authors?

WHILE YOU WATCH THE DVD, TAKE NOTES

What does the phrase "canon within the canon" mean?

the idea that there's a small piece within the whole bible (66 books) that's to be accepted → liberal idea

What kinds of books can be helpful when you encounter questions about a problem in the Bible?

Book about commonly asked questions / contradictions

What can your deep confidence in the Word of God *not* rest on? historical texts/arguments

Jesus Christ is the __________ __________ that you put in the __________ of every religion.

What analogy does John Piper give for loving something and yet not totally understanding it?

AFTER YOU WATCH THE DVD, DISCUSS WHAT YOU'VE LEARNED

1) Discuss an experience you have had where your memory failed you when you were talking to someone about the Bible. How did you respond? What would you do differently next time?

2) What are some common ways that people create Jesus in their own image? What does it mean to come to him on his own terms?

3) What difficulties have you run into while reading the Bible? Have there been any texts that have been particularly troubling? Discuss these as a group and pray together for better understanding.

AFTER YOU DISCUSS, MAKE APPLICATION

1) What was the most meaningful part of this lesson for you? Was there a sentence, a concept, or an idea that really struck you? Why? Record your thoughts in the space below.

2) Sometime this week, get together with someone you know well and ask him or her if the lifestyle choices you make reflect a hope in the future resurrection or a pursuit of earthly comfort. Furthermore, ask him or her for one or two specific areas in *your* life that are in need of change and pray together for God's help. Record your reflections below.

NOTES

1. John Piper, *What Jesus Demands from the World* (Wheaton, IL: Crossway, 2007), 77.
2. John Piper, *Desiring God* (Sisters, OR: Multnomah, 2003), 254.
3. John Piper, "Radical Effects of the Resurrection," an online article at the Desiring God Web site.
4. John Piper, "In Honor of Tethered Preaching," an online article at the Desiring God Web site.

LESSON 4

WHICH BOOKS MAKE UP THE BIBLE?

A Companion Study to the Why We Believe the Bible DVD, Session 3

LESSON OBJECTIVES

It is our prayer that after you have finished this lesson . . .

- You will understand which books make up the Old and New Testament Scriptures and why.
- You will see why the life, death, and resurrection of Jesus necessitated an expansion of the then-existing canon of Scripture.
- You will exult in God's mercy in inspiring men to write an authoritative record of his revelation for future generations.

BEFORE YOU WATCH THE DVD, STUDY AND PREPARE

DAY 1: THE OLD TESTAMENT CANON

In answering the question of whether or not the Bible is true, it is important to establish which books make up the Bible and why.

Are God's words contained in the 66 books that Protestants recognize, or is the Catholic Church correct in including the Apocrypha in their canon? Are there books we now have that should be rejected? Are there other books that are divinely inspired but haven't been discovered yet? These are significant questions. The purpose of this lesson is to help you see that the 66 books we have in our English Bibles are in fact the very words of God.

To begin, we should define what we mean by the word *canon*.

The word "canon" means straight staff, or measuring rod, and then a guide or a model or a test of truth or beauty.

GALATIANS 6:16

"And those who will walk by this rule (*kanon*), peace and mercy be upon them, and upon the Israel of God.

The earliest use is the sense of a group of books that function as a rule or measuring rod of faith and life: Council of Laodicea in AD 363 (Schaff-Herzog, I, 385):

No psalms of private authorship can be read in the churches, nor *uncanonical* books, but only the *canonical* books of the Old and New Testaments.[1]

QUESTION 1: In your own words, explain in a sentence or phrase what the term *canon* means when it is referring to Scripture. Be as concise and clear as possible.

The Divinely inspired words of God to be fully accepted as truth.

The original Hebrew Old Testament was made up of 24 books. In our English Bibles the Old Testament contains 39 books. The reason for this discrepancy is that our English Bibles have separated some books which the Hebrew Old Testament held together. Furthermore, the order of the books in the Hebrew Old Testament is different from what we have in our English translations. Knowing this will be important as we encounter some texts that help us determine which books make up the Old Testament. Read the following explanation to see this in greater detail.

> The Hebrew canon has traditionally had 24 books which include all of our 39 and no more, and these are divided into three sections: Law, Prophets, and Writings (Tanach: Torah, Nebiim, Chetuvim)
>
> Torah: Genesis, Exodus, Leviticus, Numbers, Deuteronomy
>
> Prophets: Joshua, Judges, Samuel (1/2), Kings (1/2), Isaiah, Jeremiah, Ezekiel, The Minor Prophets (= one book: Hosea, Joel, Amos, Obadiah, Jonah, Micah, Nahum, Habakkuk, Zephaniah, Haggai, Zechariah, Malachi)
>
> Writings: Psalms, Job, Proverbs, Ruth, Song of Solomon, Ecclesiastes, Lamentations, Esther, Daniel, Ezra-Nehemiah (= one book), Chronicles (1/2)
>
> Thus the canon of the Jews began with Genesis and ended with 2 Chronicles, not (as we have it today) with Malachi.[2]

With this information in mind, study Jesus' words in the following passage.

LUKE 24:44

> 44 *Then he said to them, "These are my words that I spoke to you while I was still with you, that everything written about me in the Law of Moses and the Prophets and the Psalms must be fulfilled."*

***QUESTION 2:** Circle the three divisions of Scripture Jesus names in this verse. Now attempt to match these with the three sections identified in the explanation given above. What section might Jesus be referring to when he mentions the Psalms? How does this verse help us understand which books made up the Bible Jesus used and affirmed (the Hebrew Old Testament)?

DAY 2: FROM ABEL TO ZECHARIAH

As mentioned yesterday, the Catholic Bible includes a collection of books called the Apocrypha which are not included in the Protestant Scriptures. Consider the following brief description of the Apocrypha.

> Other Jewish books besides the ones we have in our Old Testament were written after the Old Testament times. These include:
>
> The First Book of Esdras
>
> The Second Book of Esdras

Tobit

Judith

The Addition to the Book of Esther

The Wisdom of Solomon

Ecclesiasticus (or Sirach)

Baruch

The Letter of Jeremiah

The Prayer of Azariah

Suzanna

Bel and The Dragon

The Prayer of Manasseh

The First Book of the Maccabees

The Second Book of the Maccabees

The Jews did not accord to the Apocrypha the authority of the canonical books.[3]

Perhaps the most significant text for determining which books made up the Hebrew Old Testament is Luke 11:49–51. Study this text along with Genesis 4:8–10 and 2 Chronicles 24:20–21.

LUKE 11:49–51

49 Therefore also the Wisdom of God said, "I will send them prophets and apostles, some of whom they will kill and persecute," 50 so that the blood of all the prophets, shed from the foundation of the world, may be charged against this generation, 51 from the blood of Abel to the blood of Zechariah, who perished between the altar and the sanctuary. Yes, I tell you, it will be required of this generation.

GENESIS 4:8–10

8 Cain spoke to Abel his brother. And when they were in the field, Cain rose up against his brother Abel and killed him. 9 Then the LORD said to Cain, "Where is Abel your brother?" He said, "I do not know; am I my brother's keeper?" 10 And the LORD said, "What have you done? The voice of your brother's blood is crying to me from the ground."

2 CHRONICLES 24:20–21

20 Then the Spirit of God clothed Zechariah the son of Jehoiada the priest, and he stood above the people, and said to them, "Thus says God, 'Why do you break the commandments of the LORD, so that you cannot prosper? Because you have forsaken the LORD, he has forsaken you.'" 21 But they conspired against him, and by command of the king they stoned him with stones in the court of the house of the LORD.

***QUESTION 3:** Underline the two prophets Jesus mentions in Luke 11. Which book of the Bible speaks of the murder of Abel? Which book refers to the murder of Zechariah? Now, review the explanation of the original order of the books in the Hebrew canon from yesterday. What were the first and the last books in this list? Knowing this, what might we infer about which books

Jesus recognized as belonging in the Hebrew canon? What does this suggest about the Apocryphal books mentioned earlier?

Examine Jude 14–15; Acts 17:28; and Titus 1:12.

JUDE 14–15

[14] It was also about these that Enoch, the seventh from Adam, prophesied, saying, "Behold, the Lord comes with ten thousands of his holy ones, [15] to execute judgment on all and to convict all the ungodly of all their deeds of ungodliness that they have committed in such an ungodly way, and of all the harsh things that ungodly sinners have spoken against him."

ACTS 17:28

[28] For "In him we live and move and have our being"; as even some of your own poets have said, "For we are indeed his offspring."

TITUS 1:12

[12] One of the Cretans, a prophet of their own, said, "Cretans are always liars, evil beasts, lazy gluttons."

QUESTION 4: In these passages Jude quotes a noncanonical book called 1 Enoch and Paul cites pagan Greek authors. Are any of these quotations said to be from Scripture or are they presented in a way that suggests they are authoritative because of their sources? How then should we view them?

According to one count by Roger Nicole, the New Testament quotes various parts of the Old Testament as divinely authoritative over 295 times, but not once do they cite any statement from the books of the Apocrypha or any other writings as having divine authority. ("New Testament Use of the Old Testament" in *Revelation and the Bible*, ed. Carl Henry [London: Tyndale Press, 1959], pp. 137–141)[4]

DAY 3: JESUS AND THE EXPANSION OF THE CANON

During New Testament times, there was a body of authoritative literature, known as "the Scriptures," that governed the life of God's people. To see this, consider Luke 24:27; John 5:39; Acts 17:2; and Romans 15:4.

LUKE 24:27

> 27 *And beginning with Moses and all the Prophets, he interpreted to them in all the Scriptures the things concerning himself.*

JOHN 5:39

> 39 *You search the Scriptures because you think that in them you have eternal life; and it is they that bear witness about me.*

ACTS 17:2

> 2 *And Paul went in, as was his custom, and on three Sabbath days he reasoned with them from the Scriptures.*

ROMANS 15:4

> 4 *For whatever was written in former days was written for our instruction, that through endurance and through the encouragement of the Scriptures we might have hope.*

QUESTION 5: Underline every occurrence of the phrase "the Scriptures" in the passages listed above. Which portion of our current Bibles do you think this phrase encompasses? From these passages, does the idea of having a group of writings that are recognized as authoritative seem to be foreign to the Bible, or one which the Bible itself acknowledges?

When Jesus began his public ministry, he did something astounding with the existing canon of Scripture. Reflect on his teaching in Matthew 5:38–39 and Matthew's inspired interpretation of his teaching in Matthew 7:28–29.

MATTHEW 5:38–39

> 38 *You have heard that it was said, "An eye for an eye and a*
> *tooth for a tooth."* 39 *But I say to you, Do not resist the one who is evil. But if anyone slaps you on the right cheek, turn to him the other also.*

MATTHEW 7:28–29

> 28 *And when Jesus finished these sayings, the crowds were astonished at his teaching,* 29 *for he was teaching them as one who had authority, and not as their scribes.*

***QUESTION 6:** In light of Matthew's explanation of Jesus' authority, explain the significance of the phrase "But I say to you" in Matthew 5:39. What is Jesus saying about himself in relation to the Old Testament?

When Jesus finished his famous Sermon on the Mount, "the crowds were astonished at his teaching, for he was teaching them as one who had authority, and not as their scribes" (Matt. 7:28–29). This authority was not because of a personality trait or a pedagogical technique. The reason is much deeper. His words have authority and power, Jesus says, because they are the words of God. "I have not spoken on my own authority, but the Father who sent me has himself given me a commandment—what to say and what to speak" (John 12:49). "What I say, therefore, I say as the Father has told me" (John 12:50; cf. 8:28). "The word that you hear is not mine but the Father's who sent me" (John 14:24). Jesus' words have authority because when he speaks, God speaks. Jesus speaks *from* God the Father and *as* God the Son.[5]

DAY 4: THE FORMATION OF THE NEW TESTAMENT CANON

Because of the significance of Jesus' life, death, and resurrection, as well as the authority of his teachings, it would follow that there would be an enlarged body of literature that would preserve and explain these things for the sake of future generations. Read the following argument from Norman Anderson.

> If we accept [Jesus'] testimony to the God-given authority of the Old Testament, it would seem intrinsically unlikely that the most stupendous event in human history—in the life, death and resurrection of its incarnate Lord . . . would have been left by the God who had revealed it in advance without any authoritative record or explanation for future generations. (Norman Anderson, *God's Word for God's World* [London: Hodder and Stoughton, 1981], p. 124)[6]

Study the following passage.

JOHN 14:24–26

> [24] *Whoever does not love me does not keep my words. And the word that you hear is not mine but the Father's who sent me.*
> [25] *These things I have spoken to you while I am still with you.*
> [26] *But the Helper, the Holy Spirit, whom the Father will send in my name, he will teach you all things and bring to your remembrance all that I have said to you.*

***QUESTION 7:** Use your own Bible to see this passage in the context of John 13 and 14. To whom is Jesus speaking in John 14:24–26? Who does he promise the Father will send them? What will be his purpose? What does this passage tell us about how the life and teachings of Jesus will be preserved and who will be responsible for doing it?

We can see evidence that this is in fact what happened in the apostle Paul's own awareness of the authority of what he was writing. Meditate on Ephesians 2:19–20 and 1 Corinthians 14:37.

EPHESIANS 2:19–20

> [19] *So then you are no longer strangers and aliens, but you are fellow citizens with the saints and members of the household of God,* [20] *built on the foundation of the apostles and prophets, Christ Jesus himself being the cornerstone,*

1 CORINTHIANS 14:37

> [37] *If anyone thinks that he is a prophet, or spiritual, he should acknowledge that the things I am writing to you are a command of the Lord.*

QUESTION 8: What does it mean that the household of God is "built on the foundation of the apostles and prophets"? How does Paul's statement in 1 Corinthians 14:37 agree with this?

DAY 5: WHICH BOOKS MAKE UP THE NEW TESTAMENT?

The apostle Peter was also aware of the authority of Paul's writings and said something remarkable about them. Read the following passage.

2 PETER 3:15–16

15 And count the patience of our Lord as salvation, just as our beloved brother Paul also wrote to you according to the wisdom given him, 16 as he does in all his letters when he speaks in them of these matters. There are some things in them that are hard to understand, which the ignorant and unstable twist to their own destruction, as they do the other Scriptures.

QUESTION 9: Underline the phrase "the other Scriptures." How is Peter saying the writings of Paul ought to be regarded? Why is this important?

The apostles were entrusted with preserving a record of authoritative teaching for the church under the inspiration of the Holy Spirit. Read Luke 6:13–16; Acts 1:26; Galatians 1:19; and 1 Corinthians 15:7–10 to determine who these men were.

LUKE 6:13–16

13 And when day came, he called his disciples and chose from them twelve, whom he named apostles: 14 Simon, whom he named Peter, and Andrew his brother, and James and John, and Philip,

and Bartholomew, [15] and Matthew, and Thomas, and James the
son of Alphaeus, and Simon who was called the Zealot, [16] and
Judas the son of James, and Judas Iscariot, who became a traitor.

ACTS 1:26

[26] And they cast lots for them, and the lot fell on Matthias, and he was numbered with the eleven apostles.

GALATIANS 1:19

[19] But I [Paul] saw none of the other apostles except James the Lord's brother.

1 CORINTHIANS 15:7–10

[7] Then he appeared to James, then to all the apostles. [8] Last of
all, as to one untimely born, he appeared also to me. [9] For I
am the least of the apostles, unworthy to be called an apostle,
because I persecuted the church of God. [10] But by the grace of
God I am what I am, and his grace toward me was not in vain. On the contrary, I worked harder than any of them, though it was not I, but the grace of God that is with me.

***QUESTION 10:** Underline the names that are mentioned in the passages above. Now, using your own Bible, try to identify the authors of as many of the books in the New Testament as you can. Write their names in the space below. Circle which of these men are identified in the passages above as apostles. Why do you think the books written by non-apostles have been included in our New Testament canon? When you are finished, compare your answers with the list below.

The main criterion was *apostolicity*. Not just, "Was the book written by an apostle?" but also, "Was it written in the company of an apostle, presumably with his help and endorsement?"

Matthew: apostle

Mark: Peter's interpreter and assistant (Papias, Bishop of Hierapolis 60–140: "Mark became Peter's interpreter and wrote accurately all that he remembered," in Eusebius, *EH III*, 39.15)

Luke: close associate and partner of Paul (known from Acts)

John: apostle

13 epistles of Paul: apostle

Hebrews: from the Pauline circle (Hebrews 13:22–24, "But I urge you, brethren, bear with this word of exhortation, for I have written to you briefly. Take notice that *our brother Timothy* has been released, with whom, if he comes soon, I shall see you. Greet all of your leaders and all the saints. Those from Italy greet you.")

James: Jesus' brother called an apostle probably in Galatians 1:19 ("But I did not see any other of the apostles except James, the Lord's brother.")

1 & 2 Peter: apostle

1, 2, & 3 John: apostle

Jude: brother of James

Revelation: by John the apostle

The most controversial books that took the longest to confirm themselves for the whole church were Hebrews, James, 2 Peter, 2 & 3 John, and Jude. But in the end the church discerned their harmony with the others and their antiquity and essential apostolicity.[7]

FURTHER UP AND FURTHER IN

Read or listen to "How to Receive the Word of Man as the Word of God," an online sermon at the Desiring God Web site.

1 Thessalonians 2:13 is the focal point of this sermon. Meditate on this verse and then answer the following questions.

1 THESSALONIANS 2:13

> 13 *And we also thank God constantly for this, that when you received the word of God, which you heard from us, you accepted it not as the word of men but as what it really is, the word of God, which is at work in you believers.*

QUESTION 11: According to John Piper, what does it mean that the Thessalonians "received" the word of God? What does it mean that they "accepted" it? What other verse includes a similar use of the word "accepted"?

QUESTION 12: What would it look like to view the Bible as merely the word of men? How would this affect the way we interpret it?

QUESTION 13: Describe the difference between the orthodox and the neo-orthodox views of Scripture. According to the orthodox view, when the church determined which books belonged in the New Testament canon, did they bestow divine authority on these books or recognize the divine authority they already possessed?

QUESTION 14: John Piper says in this sermon that the Bible "is God's truth and has God's authority. It is the rule for all other claims to truth and the rule over all authority. We should embrace it that way." What does it look like for the Bible to rule over subjects such as mathematics, science, or psychology? Think of an example where embracing the Bible's authority would affect the way you pursue knowledge in these or other fields.

QUESTION 15: List the five M's for how to welcome the Bible as precious, pleasant, and practical. Which of the five is most difficult for you right now? Why? What practical steps can you take to pursue obedience in this area?

WHILE YOU WATCH THE DVD, TAKE NOTES

What term for the Old Testament will a Jewish person most recognize? Why?

TANACH

(includes torah, Nebiim & chetuvim)

T A N A CH

On what translation of the Old Testament is the order of the books in our English Old Testament based? What is the name for this translation?

the Greek translation ?

Chronologically, the last martyr in the Old Testament was URIAH the son of Shemaiah (Jeremiah 26:20–23).

Jesus' bible was the Hebrew canon (not including the apocrypha)

2 Chron 24:20-21 (would've been the end of the scriptures then)

The word *apostle* means "a sent one who goes with ______________ ______________ of another."

Explain John Piper's application of C. S. Lewis's "Liar, Lunatic, or Lord" argument to the authority the apostle Paul claims for himself in 1 Corinthians 14:37.

AFTER YOU WATCH THE DVD, DISCUSS WHAT YOU'VE LEARNED

1) What did you learn about the books which make up our Bible that you didn't know before? How was this helpful to you?

2) Does it bother you that Jude quotes from the non-canonical book of 1 Enoch? As a group, revisit the reasons for not concluding from this quotation that 1 Enoch is inspired Scripture. Work through any questions that remain.

3) Suppose someone came up to you and claimed to have received new, authoritative revelation from God. From what you have just learned in this lesson, explain how you would respond to this person. What Biblical texts would you use to demonstrate that the canon is now closed?

AFTER YOU DISCUSS, MAKE APPLICATION

1) What was the most meaningful part of this lesson for you? Was there a sentence, concept, or idea that really struck you? Why? Record your thoughts in the space below.

- It was neat when Jesus referenced Abel to Zechariah & the implications of that.

2) If you have not already done this, set aside time this week to memorize the books of the Bible in order. If you have already committed them to memory, recite them several times during the week. Knowing the books of the Bible in order will be a great help to you as you study the Scriptures.

NOTES

1. John Piper, "Why We Believe the Bible, Part 1," an online resource at the Desiring God Web site.
2. John Piper, "Why We Believe the Bible, Part 1," an online resource at the Desiring God Web site.
3. John Piper, "Why We Believe the Bible, Part 1," an online resource at the Desiring God Web site.
4. John Piper, "Why We Believe the Bible, Part 1," an online resource at the Desiring God Web site.
5. John Piper, *What Jesus Demands from the World*, (Wheaton, IL: Crossway, 2007), 57.
6. John Piper, "Why We Believe the Bible, Part 1," an online resource at the Desiring God Web site.
7. John Piper, "Why We Believe the Bible, Part 1," an online resource at the Desiring God Web site.

LESSON 5

DO WE HAVE THE VERY WORDS WRITTEN BY THE BIBLICAL AUTHORS?

A Companion Study to the Why We Believe the Bible DVD, Session 4

LESSON OBJECTIVES

It is our prayer that after you have finished this lesson . . .

- You will have gained a preliminary understanding of the issues involved in textual criticism.
- You will have a settled assurance that our current Bibles contain the very words of God.
- You will praise God for his faithfulness in preserving a trustworthy record of his revelation over thousands of years.

BEFORE YOU WATCH THE DVD, STUDY AND PREPARE

DAY 1: RIGHT BOOKS, WRONG TEXT?

In the last lesson, you examined which books make up the canon of Scripture and saw evidence for concluding that all 66 books in

.r English Bibles bear the authority of God, no more, no less. However, another question remains. How can we be sure that the current words we possess are in fact the words the original authors wrote? After all, it makes little difference that we have the right books if the content of those books has been distorted. The purpose of this lesson, then, is to address the issues related to this important question so that we might have confidence in the text our English Bibles contain.

To begin, study 1 Timothy 5:17–18. This passage will serve as a bridge between the previous lesson and this lesson.

1 TIMOTHY 5:17–18

> 17 *Let the elders who rule well be considered worthy of double honor, especially those who labor in preaching and teaching.*
> 18 *For the Scripture says, "You shall not muzzle an ox when it treads out the grain," and, "The laborer deserves his wages."*

Now, examine the two passages Paul is quoting here: Deuteronomy 25:4 and Luke 10:7.

DEUTERONOMY 25:4

> 4 *You shall not muzzle an ox when it is treading out the grain.*

LUKE 10:7

> 7 *And remain in the same house, eating and drinking what they provide, for the laborer deserves his wages. Do not go from house to house.*

QUESTION 1: From the previous lesson, what was the main criterion for whether a New Testament book was considered to be inspired by God? Was Luke an apostle? Why is it significant that

Paul pairs Deuteronomy 25:4 and Luke 10:7 together and calls them both "Scripture"?

***QUESTION 2:** How do you think the words Moses wrote in Deuteronomy 25:4 were preserved over a thousand years for Paul to receive and quote? In other words, did Paul have the original document on which Moses wrote? How is Paul's situation similar to ours?

DAY 2: WITHOUT ERROR IN THE ORIGINAL MANUSCRIPTS

The initial document which a biblical author wrote is often called the "original manuscript." Today, we have no original manuscript of any biblical book, not even a fragment. Our present Bible is the product of many copies of other copies of the original manuscripts. With this in mind, read this excerpt from section 1 of the BBC Elder Affirmation of Faith, entitled "Scripture, the Word of God Written."

> 1.1 We believe that the Bible, consisting of the sixty-six books of the Old and New Testaments, is the infallible Word

of God, verbally inspired by God, and without error in the original manuscripts.[1]

***QUESTION 3:** Why do you think it is important to affirm that the Bible is without error "in the original manuscripts"? What does this imply about the Scriptures we currently possess?

QUESTION 4: How does it make you feel to know that we do not possess the original biblical manuscripts? Do you think it is still possible to be confident that the Scriptures we now have are, in fact, the words of God? Explain.

DAY 3: IN A LEAGUE OF ITS OWN

Today, we possess well over five-thousand manuscripts, or copies, of the New Testament writings. Some contain portions of texts, while others contain larger segments. Compare this number to the number of manuscripts we have of other works from the New Testament era.

We have no original manuscripts of any other writers from this period of history.

Moreover the textual evidence of other writings cannot compare with the wealth of New Testament manuscripts. For example:

Caesar's *Gallic Wars* (composed between 58 and 50 BC). There are about 10 manuscripts available and the oldest is 900 years after the event.

Parts of the *Roman History* of Livy (composed between 59 BC and AD 17) is preserved in about 20 manuscripts, only one of which, containing only fragments, is as old as the fourth century.

The *Histories* and the *Annals* of the Roman historian Tacitus (composed around AD 100) are preserved (partially) only in two manuscripts, one from the ninth and one from the eleventh century.

The *History* of Thucydides (who lived 460–400 BC) is known to us from only eight manuscripts, the earliest belonging to AD 900, and a few papyrus scraps from the beginning of the Christian era.

The same general picture is true of Herodotus (who lived about 480–425 BC).[2]

QUESTION 5: How might these statistics increase your confidence in the Bible? What does the magnitude of New Testament manuscripts tell us about how the ancient church valued the preservation of the original words of Scripture?

***QUESTION 6:** Do you think having so many manuscripts increases or decreases accuracy when we try to determine the original biblical text? Why?

The huge number of manuscripts of the New Testament results in two things: 1) there are *many variations* in wording among them because they were all copied by hand and subject to human error; 2) there are so many manuscripts that these *errors tend to be self-correcting* by the many manuscript witnesses we have to compare.[3]

DAY 4: TYPES OF COPYING ERRORS

There are two main categories of errors people made when copying the Scriptures. The first category is *unintentional* errors. This includes such mistakes as confusing vowel sounds, skipping from one word to another identical word at a different location, and changing the order of letters or words. These are common errors that we make even today when we copy a paragraph out of a book or try to write down the words a person is speaking.

To see an example of an unintentional error, read Romans 5:1. Remember, when we speak of errors in this lesson we are referring to errors in copying, not errors in the original manuscripts.

ROMANS 5:1

> [1] *Therefore, since we have been justified by faith, we have peace with God through our Lord Jesus Christ.*

The ESV footnote for this verse explains that some manuscripts have "let us" instead of "we" in the phrase "we have peace with God." In the original language the words for "we have" and "let us have" are identical except for one similar vowel sound.

***QUESTION 7:** What is the difference in meaning between the two possible wordings for this verse? Which wording do you think agrees most with Paul's flow of thought in this verse and its broader context?

The second category of copying errors is *intentional* errors. These occur where the copyist, likely without malicious intent, tried to alter the text to agree more with a parallel passage, to better reflect the language of an Old Testament text being quoted, or to correct what seemed to be a factual error.

To see an example of this type of error, study Mark 1:2–3 in light of Malachi 3:1 and Isaiah 40:2–3.

MARK 1:2–3

> [2] *As it is written in Isaiah the prophet, "Behold, I send my messenger before your face, who will prepare your way,* [3] *the voice of one crying in the wilderness: 'Prepare the way of the Lord, make his paths straight.'"*

MALACHI 3:1

> [1] *"Behold, I send my messenger, and he will prepare the way before me. And the Lord whom you seek will suddenly come to his temple; and the messenger of the covenant in whom you delight, behold, he is coming, says the* LORD *of hosts.*

ISAIAH 40:2–3

> [2] *Speak tenderly to Jerusalem, and cry to her that her warfare is ended, that her iniquity is pardoned, that she has received from the* LORD*'s hand double for all her sins.* [3] *A voice cries: "In the wilderness prepare the way of the* LORD*; make straight in the desert a highway for our God."*

Notice the phrase "in Isaiah the prophet" in Mark 1:2. This is the wording with the best support from the manuscripts. However, the ESV footnote for this phrase explains that some manuscripts replace the phrase "in Isaiah the prophet" with the phrase "in the prophets."

QUESTION 8: As you compare the quotation in Mark 1:2–3 with Malachi 3:1 and Isaiah 40:2–3, why do you think some copyists were tempted to change the text to say "in the prophets"?

DAY 5: TEXTUAL CRITICISM

The branch of biblical studies that attempts to discern, from the available manuscripts, the original words of Scripture is called "textual criticism." The church owes a great debt to those who have given their lives to this work so that we might have a text of Scripture that is reliable and as close to the original wording as possible.

One of the more famous passages involving textual criticism is John 7:53–8:11. Find this passage in your own Bible and answer the following question.

QUESTION 9: Record below any notes your Bible gives for this section. Is there anything in John 7:53–8:11 that disagrees with other passages of Scripture? What would be the implications if this passage were not originally a part of John's gospel? Is there any major doctrine or biblical truth at stake if we understand this story to have been absent from the original text?

> The variant readings about which any doubt remains among textual critics of the New Testament affects no material question of historic fact or of Christian faith and practice. (F. F. Bruce, *The New Testament Documents*, p. 20)[4]

***QUESTION 10:** Briefly skim your Bible looking for footnotes about alternative wordings in some manuscripts. Do these notes dominate the biblical text, or are they more of a minor component? Where there are variations, do they change the meaning of the text substantially? Because of this, do you think it is possible to have confidence that our Bibles contain the inspired words of God?

Wayne Grudem provides some very helpful concluding comments.

> It may first be stated that for over 99 percent of the words of the Bible, we *know* what the original manuscript said. Even for many of the verses where there are textual variants (that is, different words in different ancient copies of the same verse), the correct decision is often quite clear, and there are really very few places where the textual variant is both difficult to evaluate and significant in determining the meaning. In the small percentage of cases where there is significant uncertainty about what the original text said, the general sense of the sentence is usually quite clear from the context. (One does not have to be a Hebrew or Greek scholar to know where these variants are, because all modern English translations indicate them in marginal notes with words such as "some ancient manuscripts read . . . " or "other ancient authorities add . . . ")
>
> This is not to say that the study of textual variants is unimportant, but it is to say that the study of textual variants has not left us in confusion about what the original manuscripts said. It has rather brought us extremely close to the content of those original manuscripts. For most practical purposes,

> then, the *current published scholarly texts* of the Hebrew Old Testament and Greek New Testament *are the same as the original manuscripts*. Thus, when we say that the original manuscripts were inerrant, we are also implying that over 99 percent of the words in our present manuscripts are also inerrant, for they are exact copies of the originals. Furthermore, we *know* where the uncertain readings are (for where there are no textual variants we have no reason to expect faulty copying of the original). Thus, our present manuscripts are for most purposes the same as the original manuscripts, and the doctrine of inerrancy therefore directly concerns our present manuscripts as well.[5]

FURTHER UP AND FURTHER IN

Our English Bibles are translations from Greek and Hebrew manuscripts. Because of this, it is important not only to determine which words were written by the original authors, but also to decide how those words should be translated when they are brought over into English. The following article addresses this very issue.

Read "Good English with Minimal Translation: Why Bethlehem Uses the ESV," an online article at the Desiring God Web site.

QUESTION 11: Which translations of the Bible have you used over the years? Which do you currently use? What do you like about it? What do you wish were different, if anything?

QUESTION 12: Explain the comparison between loving the Bible and loving your eyes. Do you think this is a helpful illustration? Why or why not?

QUESTION 13: John Piper writes in this article, "Ten thousand benefits flow from the influence of this book that we are not even aware of. And the preaching of this Word in tens of thousands of pulpits across America is more important than every media outlet in the nation." What do you think are some of these "ten thousand benefits"? Explain briefly why the preaching of the Word is "more important than every media outlet in the nation."

QUESTION 14: Ponder the comparison between the NASB and the NIV. In light of this, what seems to be the greatest tension in translating from the original documents to English? What are the benefits and dangers of emphasizing one side of the tension over the other?

QUESTION 15: Study the example of John 11:1–6 in the ESV and NIV. Why is the difference in the wording of verse 6 so significant? How does the ESV show here that "Jesus' delay is an *expression* of love for Mary and Martha and Lazarus"?

WHILE YOU WATCH THE DVD, TAKE NOTES

According to Dr. Goppelt, why shouldn't we go back to the first two or three centuries of the church to look for a more accurate theology?

Which books of the New Testament were the most controversial and took the longest to confirm themselves for the whole church?

In what year was the first printed Greek New Testament?

How many manuscript fragments of the Greek New Testament do we have today?

The documents that we have in front of us in our Greek New Testament are considered to be _______________ by the most liberal German scholars.

AFTER YOU WATCH THE DVD, DISCUSS WHAT YOU'VE LEARNED

1) When you think about whether or not we have the words the original biblical authors wrote, do you have any remaining questions? Discuss these as a group.

2) What are some implications of the fact that God determined to have his Word be preserved and transmitted

by fallible human copyists? What would be lost if God simply dropped a book out of the sky every generation or so?

3) Do you think it is necessary for every Christian to know Greek and Hebrew in order to be confident that their Bibles contain the very words of God? If so, why? If not, why not? Who then should learn?

AFTER YOU DISCUSS, MAKE APPLICATION

1) What was the most meaningful part of this lesson for you? Was there a sentence, a concept, or an idea that really struck you? Why? Record your thoughts in the space below.

2) Devote a portion of your prayer time this week to asking that God would raise up and send Bible translators to people groups that do not have the Word of God available in their heart language. What can you do to promote this undertaking? Record your reflections below.

NOTES

1. The Bethlehem Baptist Church Elder Affirmation of Faith with Scripture proofs can be accessed at http://hopeingod.org/resources/images/1230.pdf.
2. John Piper, "Why We Believe the Bible, Part 1," an online resource at the Desiring God Web site.
3. John Piper, "Why We Believe the Bible, Part 1," an online resource at the Desiring God Web site.
4. John Piper, "Why We Believe the Bible, Part 1," an online resource at the Desiring God Web site.
5. Wayne Grudem, *Systematic Theology* (Grand Rapids: Zondervan, 1994), 96.

LESSON 6

WHAT DOES THE BIBLE CLAIM FOR ITSELF?

A Companion Study to the Why We Believe the Bible DVD, Session 5

LESSON OBJECTIVES

It is our prayer that after you have finished this lesson . . .

- You will be able to better articulate how Jesus viewed the Old Testament.
- You will desire to fight temptation as Jesus did by memorizing portions of the Bible.
- You will worship Jesus because of his glad obedience to all that the Scriptures had foretold concerning him.

BEFORE YOU WATCH THE DVD, STUDY AND PREPARE

DAY 1: WRITING WITH THE AUTHORITY OF GOD

The last two lessons have been devoted to establishing the reliability of the books and words that make up our Bibles. With this in place, it is now fitting to examine the claims the Bible makes for itself. More particularly, we will interact with Jesus' view of the Old Testament Scriptures. To that end, this lesson will comprise a survey of relevant biblical texts which demonstrate Jesus' high regard for the written Word of God.

First, study Psalm 110:1 and Mark 12:35–37.

PSALM 110:1

> [1] *The LORD says to my Lord: "Sit at my right hand, until I make your enemies your footstool."*

MARK 12:35–37

> [35] *And as Jesus taught in the temple, he said, "How can the scribes say that the Christ is the son of David?* [36] *David himself, in the Holy Spirit, declared, 'The Lord said to my Lord, Sit at my right hand, until I put your enemies under your feet.'*
> [37] *David himself calls him Lord. So how is he his son?" And the great throng heard him gladly.*

QUESTION 1: Who are the two Lords in Psalm 110:1? How does Jesus understand himself in light of this verse in Mark 12:35–37? What phrase in Jesus' statement indicates his view of David's authority in writing Psalm 110:1? What does this phrase mean?

Meditate on Genesis 2:22–25 and Matthew 19:3–6.

GENESIS 2:22–25

> [22] *And the rib that the* Lord *God had taken from the man he*
> *made into a woman and brought her to the man.* [23] *Then the*
> *man said, "This at last is bone of my bones and flesh of my flesh;*
> *she shall be called Woman, because she was taken out of Man."*
> [24] *Therefore a man shall leave his father and his mother and hold*
> *fast to his wife, and they shall become one flesh.* [25] *And the man*
> *and his wife were both naked and were not ashamed.*

MATTHEW 19:3–6

> [3] *And Pharisees came up to him and tested him by asking, "Is*
> *it lawful to divorce one's wife for any cause?"* [4] *He answered,*
> *"Have you not read that he who created them from the begin-*
> *ning made them male and female,* [5] *and said, 'Therefore a man*
> *shall leave his father and his mother and hold fast to his wife,*
> *and the two shall become one flesh'?* [6] *So they are no longer two*
> *but one flesh. What therefore God has joined together, let not*
> *man separate."*

***QUESTION 2:** Is Genesis 2:24 a quotation of God's speech or a comment made by Moses, the author? Who, according to Jesus in Matthew 9:4–5, spoke the words of Genesis 2:24? What does this suggest about Jesus' view of Moses' authority?

One small but powerful example that Jesus thought all of the Old Testament Scriptures were God's words is the way he responded to the Pharisees when they tested him by asking, "Is it lawful to divorce one's wife for any cause?" He answered by referring back to Genesis 2:24 where Moses wrote—*Moses* wrote this; it's not a quotation from God—"a man shall leave his father and his mother and hold fast to his wife, and they shall become one flesh."

So Jesus answers the Pharisees' question like this: "Have you not read that he who created them from the beginning made them male and female and said . . . " Now who is doing the "saying" here? The one who made them male and female—God. So let's start over and listen to the implication of Jesus' saying *God* said this: "Have you not read that he who created them from the beginning made them male and female, and said [then he quotes what *Moses* said, Genesis 2:24], 'Therefore a man shall leave his father and his mother and hold fast to his wife, and they shall become one flesh'?" In other words, Jesus can take any seemingly random Scripture—like Genesis 2:24, written by Moses—and say, "God said it."[1]

DAY 2: SUFFICIENT FOR FIGHTING TEMPTATION

Because Jesus saw the Old Testament as possessing the very authority of God, he used it to fight against Satan's temptations in the wilderness. Read the account of these temptations in the following passage.

MATTHEW 4:1–11

> [1] *Then Jesus was led up by the Spirit into the wilderness to be*
> *tempted by the devil.* [2] *And after fasting forty days and forty*
> *nights, he was hungry.* [3] *And the tempter came and said to him,*
> *"If you are the Son of God, command these stones to become*

*loaves of bread." 4 But he answered, "It is written, 'Man shall
not live by bread alone, but by every word that comes from the
mouth of God.'" 5 Then the devil took him to the holy city and
set him on the pinnacle of the temple 6 and said to him, "If you
are the Son of God, throw yourself down, for it is written, 'He
will command his angels concerning you,' and 'On their hands
they will bear you up, lest you strike your foot against a stone.'"
7 Jesus said to him, "Again it is written, 'You shall not put the
Lord your God to the test.'" 8 Again, the devil took him to a very
high mountain and showed him all the kingdoms of the world
and their glory. 9 And he said to him, "All these I will give you,
if you will fall down and worship me." 10 Then Jesus said to
him, "Be gone, Satan! For it is written, 'You shall worship the
Lord your God and him only shall you serve.'" 11 Then the devil
left him, and behold, angels came and were ministering to him.*

***QUESTION 3:** In each of the three temptations, what had Jesus come to earth to do that Satan was trying to have him avoid? How did Jesus defeat these temptations? What does this reveal about the authority of the Scriptures compared to the authority of Satan and the authority of Jesus' human preferences?

QUESTION 4: Using your own Bible, locate the Old Testament reference for each of the verses Jesus uses in responding to Satan. From which book do they all come? How do you think Jesus had access to these verses in the wilderness? What should we learn from this about our own fight against temptation?

John Piper relates his own experience of the importance of memorizing Scripture.

> How shall we use the Word of God to fight for joy? The first answer I have given is to read it with plan and regularity. The next answer I give is to memorize verses and paragraphs and chapters and even whole books of the Bible. The older you get, the harder it is. I am fifty-eight as I write this, and I still invest significant time in memorizing Scripture, but it is much harder now than it used to be. It takes far more repetition to make the words stick to this aging brain.
>
> But I would not give it up any more than a miser would give up his stash of gold. I feel the same way Dallas Willard does when he says:
>
> Bible memorization is absolutely fundamental to spiritual formation. If I had to choose between all the disciplines of the spiritual life, I would choose Bible memorization, because it is a fundamental way of filling our mind with what it needs. This book of the law shall not depart out of your mouth. That's where you need it! How does it get in your mouth? Memorization.
>
> The joy-producing effects of memorizing Scripture and having it in my head and heart are incalculable. The world and its God-ignoring, all-embracing secularism is pervasive. It invades my mind every day. What hope is there to have a mind filled with Christ except to have a mind filled with his Word? I know of no alternative.[2]

DAY 3: THE SCRIPTURE CANNOT BE BROKEN

Jesus made an astounding claim about the Old Testament in telling the story of Lazarus and the rich man. Study the following passage to see this.

LUKE 16:27–31

> [27] *And he [the rich man] said, "Then I beg you, father [Abraham],*
> *to send him [Lazarus] to my father's house—* [28] *for I have five*
> *brothers—so that he may warn them, lest they also come into*
> *this place of torment."* [29] *But Abraham said, "They have Moses*
> *and the Prophets; let them hear them."* [30] *And he said, "No,*
> *father Abraham, but if someone goes to them from the dead,*
> *they will repent."* [31] *He said to him, "If they do not hear Moses*
> *and the Prophets, neither will they be convinced if someone*
> *should rise from the dead."*

QUESTION 5: How do Moses and the Prophets warn about the torment the rich man was experiencing? Why is this testimony more compelling than someone rising from the dead and speaking?

> Then comes Abraham's final, utterly stunning statement (v. 31): "If they do not hear Moses and the prophets, neither will they be convinced if someone should rise from the dead." Isn't that incredible! If a person is so in love with money that he is deaf to the commands and warnings and promises of Moses and the prophets, then even a resurrection from the dead will not bring about repentance.

> So here we have the same point that we saw earlier in verse 14, only here it's intensified because of the resurrection. Suppose Jesus should rise from the dead—this is what Luke wants his readers to think about—and suppose he should reveal himself to five brothers like these. Will they receive him for who he is?
>
> O, they might be utterly knocked out of their senses by the miracle of an irrefutable resurrection. But the question is, Will they be knocked out of their sins? Will they repent? Abraham says no. They will not repent. Why not? What will keep them from receiving Jesus for the financial radical that he really is? Answer: the love of money, the love of things.[3]

Study Psalm 82:6–7 and John 10:33–36.

PSALM 82:6–7

> *6 I said, "You are gods, sons of the Most High, all of you; 7 nevertheless, like men you shall die, and fall like any prince."*

JOHN 10:33–36

> *33 The Jews answered him, "It is not for a good work that we are going to stone you but for blasphemy, because you, being a man, make yourself God." 34 Jesus answered them, "Is it not written in your Law, 'I said, you are gods'? 35 If he called them gods to whom the word of God came—and Scripture cannot be broken— 36 do you say of him whom the Father consecrated and sent into the world, 'You are blaspheming,' because I said, 'I am the Son of God'?"*

***QUESTION 6:** How does Jesus use Psalm 82:6 against the Pharisees? What is his argument from this text? What does this demonstrate about how he regarded even the smallest statements of Scripture?

DAY 4: THE WORD OF GOD AND HUMAN TRADITIONS

Examine Mark 7:9–13 to see Jesus' response to the traditions of the Pharisees and the scribes.

MARK 7:9–13

> [9] *And he said to them, "You have a fine way of rejecting the commandment of God in order to establish your tradition!*
> [10] *For Moses said, 'Honor your father and your mother'; and, 'Whoever reviles father or mother must surely die.'* [11] *But you*
> *say, 'If a man tells his father or his mother, "Whatever you would have gained from me is Corban"' (that is, given to God)—* [12] *then*
> *you no longer permit him to do anything for his father or mother,*
> [13] *thus making void the word of God by your tradition that you have handed down. And many such things you do."*

QUESTION 7: From reading this passage, what do you understand about the tradition of Corban? How did this tradition violate the commandment of God? Are there any traditions you can think of today that do the same thing?

Observe the intended effect of the Old Testament Scriptures in the following passage.

MARK 12:18–27

*18 And Sadducees came to him, who say that there is no resur-
rection. And they asked him a question, saying, 19 "Teacher,
Moses wrote for us that if a man's brother dies and leaves a
wife, but leaves no child, the man must take the widow and
raise up offspring for his brother. 20 There were seven brothers;
the first took a wife, and when he died left no offspring. 21 And
the second took her, and died, leaving no offspring. And the
third likewise. 22 And the seven left no offspring. Last of all the
woman also died. 23 In the resurrection, when they rise again,
whose wife will she be? For the seven had her as wife." 24 Jesus
said to them, "Is this not the reason you are wrong, because
you know neither the Scriptures nor the power of God? 25 For
when they rise from the dead, they neither marry nor are given
in marriage, but are like angels in heaven. 26 And as for the
dead being raised, have you not read in the book of Moses, in
the passage about the bush, how God spoke to him, saying, 'I
am the God of Abraham, and the God of Isaac, and the God
of Jacob'? 27 He is not God of the dead, but of the living. You
are quite wrong."*

***QUESTION 8:** According to Jesus, why were the Sadducees wrong about the resurrection? How do the Scriptures guard us from error today? Try to think of an example in your own life where you experienced the Bible's correcting power and briefly describe it below.

DAY 5: FULFILLING THE SCRIPTURES

Study Luke 4:16–21; John 13:18–19; Mark 14:26–28; Luke 22:36–37; and Luke 24:25–27.

LUKE 4:16–21

*[16] And he came to Nazareth, where he had been brought up.
And as was his custom, he went to the synagogue on the Sabbath
day, and he stood up to read. [17] And the scroll of the prophet
Isaiah was given to him. He unrolled the scroll and found the
place where it was written, [18] "The Spirit of the Lord is upon
me, because he has anointed me to proclaim good news to the
poor. He has sent me to proclaim liberty to the captives and
recovering of sight to the blind, to set at liberty those who are
oppressed, [19] to proclaim the year of the Lord's favor." [20] And
he rolled up the scroll and gave it back to the attendant and sat
down. And the eyes of all in the synagogue were fixed on him.
[21] And he began to say to them, "Today this Scripture has been
fulfilled in your hearing."*

JOHN 13:18–19

*[18] I am not speaking of all of you; I know whom I have chosen.
But the Scripture will be fulfilled, "He who ate my bread has
lifted his heel against me." [19] I am telling you this now, before
it takes place, that when it does take place you may believe that
I am he.*

MARK 14:26–28

*[26] And when they had sung a hymn, they went out to the Mount
of Olives. [27] And Jesus said to them, "You will all fall away,
for it is written, 'I will strike the shepherd, and the sheep will
be scattered.' [28] But after I am raised up, I will go before you
to Galilee."*

LUKE 22:36–37

> [36] *He said to them, "But now let the one who has a moneybag take it, and likewise a knapsack. And let the one who has no sword sell his cloak and buy one.* [37] *For I tell you that this Scripture must be fulfilled in me: 'And he was numbered with the transgressors.' For what is written about me has its fulfillment."*

LUKE 24:25–27

> [25] *And he said to them, "O foolish ones, and slow of heart to believe all that the prophets have spoken!* [26] *Was it not necessary that the Christ should suffer these things and enter into his glory?"* [27] *And beginning with Moses and all the Prophets, he interpreted to them in all the Scriptures the things concerning himself.*

***QUESTION 9:** In examining these passages, how did the Old Testament inform Jesus' understanding of his life and ministry? Can you think of other Old Testament Scriptures that spoke about what Jesus would do and be like?

QUESTION 10: From what you have seen in this lesson, write a brief explanation of how Jesus viewed the written Word of God.

> The diversity of this witness and its spread over all the Gospel material show that the Lord Jesus regarded the Old Testament as a trustworthy, authoritative, unerring guide in our quest for enduring happiness. Therefore, we who submit to the authority of Christ will also want to submit to the authority of the book He esteemed so highly.[4]

FURTHER UP AND FURTHER IN

Read or listen to "Jesus Is Precious Because His Biblical Portrait Is True, Part 2," an online sermon at the Desiring God Web site.

QUESTION 11: What is the relationship between trusting Jesus and accepting the Bible as the inerrant Word of God? Which typically happens first? Have you found this to be true in your own life?

John Piper remarks on John 2:23–25. Study this passage and then answer the question below.

JOHN 2:23–25

> [23] *Now when he was in Jerusalem at the Passover Feast, many*
> *believed in his name when they saw the signs that he was doing.*
> [24] *But Jesus on his part did not entrust himself to them, because*
> *he knew all people* [25] *and needed no one to bear witness about*
> *man, for he himself knew what was in man.*

QUESTION 12: Explain what John means when he says "many believed in his name." Is this a saving faith? How do you know? Can you think of an example today that would demonstrate this kind of "believing"?

QUESTION 13: What was the soul of all of Jesus' miracles? How is perceiving this soul both the basis of and the hindrance to genuine saving faith?

QUESTION 14: List the three options that explain how the biblical authors could have presented a unified portrayal of the person of Jesus. Interact with each in your own words as if you were trying to explain this to an unbelieving family member or friend. Which one is the most persuasive and why?

QUESTION 15: How did Jesus view the Old and New Testaments? Why is it important to ask this question?

WHILE YOU WATCH THE DVD, TAKE NOTES

Why does John Piper focus on Jesus' view of the Old Testament rather than the testimony of the apostles, the prophets, and the Law?

Is it true to say that young people don't have any traditions yet? Why or why not?

Why is the passage in Mark 12 about the woman who had been married seven times relevant to today?

Jesus believed that everything that he did and that John the Baptist did—his whole life—was laid out for him in the ______________ ______________.

Why does the prophecy about the disciples' abandonment of Jesus create a theological challenge?

AFTER YOU WATCH THE DVD, DISCUSS WHAT YOU'VE LEARNED

1) Discuss the story of Lazarus and the rich man in Luke 16. Why is it tempting to believe that a spectacular event such as someone's coming back from the dead would be more compelling than the testimony of Scripture? Why is this not an accurate belief? How should this affect our own approach to Scripture and our use of it in evangelism?

2) What role has fulfilled prophecy played in your coming to faith in Christ and your continued confidence in who he is? How does the Old Testament point to Jesus? Spend some time as a group searching for and discussing texts that anticipate a coming Redeemer.

3) In what areas of your life are you "slow of heart" to believe what the Bible has spoken? Devote time to praying for breakthroughs in one another's lives.

AFTER YOU DISCUSS, MAKE APPLICATION

1) What was the most meaningful part of this lesson for you? Was there a sentence, a concept, or an idea that really struck you? Why? Record your thoughts in the space below.

2) Identify an area of your life where you are most tempted to sin. Select a passage of Scripture that addresses this temptation and memorize it this week for your own fight of faith (1 Timothy 6:12). How were you helped by having this passage in your heart? Record your reflections below.

NOTES

1. John Piper, "Thank God for an Inspired Bible," an online sermon at the Desiring God Web site.
2. John Piper, *When I Don't Desire God*, 119.
3. John Piper, "Preparing to Receive Christ: Hearing Moses and the Prophets," an online sermon at the Desiring God Web site.
4. John Piper, *Desiring God* (Sisters, OR: Multnomah, 2003), 333.

LESSON 7

HOW CAN WE JUSTIFY THE CLAIM THAT THE BIBLE IS GOD'S WORD? (PART 1)

A Companion Study to the Why We Believe the Bible DVD, Session 6

LESSON OBJECTIVES

It is our prayer that after you have finished this lesson . . .

- › You will have begun to formulate a reasonable defense of the authority of the Bible.
- › You will see the unique majesty of the Scriptures in comparison to all other writings.
- › You will cry out to God with childlike dependence, asking him to give you greater visions of his glory in Christ through reading the Word.

BEFORE YOU WATCH THE DVD, STUDY AND PREPARE

DAY 1: DEFENDING THE BIBLE'S AUTHORITY

The purpose of the previous lesson was to present Jesus' view of the Old Testament, and by implication, what the whole Bible claims for itself. You saw that Jesus understood the Old Testament as possessing unbreakable authority as God's revelation. It is now fitting to ask why we should hold the same view. How do we defend the Bible's claim to be the inspired Word of God? This lesson will introduce you to the first two evidences provided by the Westminster Larger Catechism.

***QUESTION 1:** If you were given 5 minutes to defend the authority of the Bible, what would you say? How have you come to believe that the Bible is God's Word?

QUESTION 2: Do you think a new believer in a remote tribe with no resource but the Bible in his or her language could adequately argue for the reliability of the Scriptures? What would that look like?

DAY 2: THIS GLORIOUS BOOK

Interact with the following excerpt from the Westminster Confession of Faith to see how the church has argued for the truthfulness of Scripture in the past.

> 1.5 We may be moved and induced by the testimony of the Church to an high and reverent esteem of the Holy Scripture, and the heavenliness of the matter, the efficacy of the doctrine, the majesty of the style, the consent of all the parts, the scope of the whole, (which is to give all glory to God), the full discovery it makes of the only way of man's salvation, the many other incomparable excellencies, and the entire perfection thereof, are arguments whereby it doth abundantly evidence itself to be the Word of God; yet, notwithstanding, our full persuasion and assurance of the infallible truth, and divine authority thereof, is from the inward work of the Holy Spirit, bearing witness by and with the word in our hearts.[1]

QUESTION 3: Underline two arguments for the Bible's being the Word of God from this paragraph (e.g., "the efficacy of the doctrine") and briefly explain what you think these arguments mean. How do they persuade a person that the Scriptures are God-breathed?

***QUESTION 4:** What is the "inward work of the Holy Spirit"? How does it relate to the arguments that have been outlined in the Westminster Confession of Faith? Does it render them unnecessary? Explain.

DAY 3: THE MAJESTY OF THE SCRIPTURES

The Westminster Larger Catechism distills the evidences for the reliability of the Scriptures into a six-part answer to the question, "How doth it appear that the Scriptures are the Word of God?"

> Question Four: How doth it appear that the Scriptures are the Word of God?
>
> Answer: The Scriptures manifest themselves to be the Word of God,
>
> 1. by their majesty
>
> 2. and purity;
>
> 3. by the consent of all the parts,
>
> 4. and the scope of the whole, which is to give all glory to God;
>
> 5. by their light and power to convince and convert sinners, to comfort and build up believers unto salvation.
>
> 6. But the Spirit of God, bearing witness by and with the Scriptures in the heart of man, is alone able fully to persuade it that they are the very Word of God.[2]

We will begin by examining the first answer: "by their majesty."

***QUESTION 5:** In what way are the Scriptures majestic? Can you think of any texts from the Bible that have struck you with their majesty?

Study the following passage.

1 CORINTHIANS 2:6–9

> 6 *Yet among the mature we do impart wisdom, although it is*
> *not a wisdom of this age or of the rulers of this age, who are*
> *doomed to pass away.* 7 *But we impart a secret and hidden wis-*
> *dom of God, which God decreed before the ages for our glory.*
> 8 *None of the rulers of this age understood this, for if they had,*
> *they would not have crucified the Lord of glory.* 9 *But, as it is*
> *written, "What no eye has seen, nor ear heard, nor the heart*
> *of man imagined, what God has prepared for those who love*
> *him"* . . .

QUESTION 6: How does Paul describe what he imparts among the mature? What distinguishes this wisdom from the "wisdom of this age"? How does this text contribute to our understanding of the majesty of the Bible?

DAY 4: WONDROUS THINGS OUT OF YOUR LAW

The Psalms likewise extol the majesty of the Word of God. To see this, read Psalm 119:18 and Psalm 119:129.

PSALM 119:18

> [18] *Open my eyes, that I may behold wondrous things out of your law.*

PSALM 119:129

> [129] *Your testimonies are wonderful; therefore my soul keeps them.*

QUESTION 7: According to these verses, what drives our obedience to the testimonies of God? How do we come to see the wonder of the Scriptures? What keeps us from seeing this wonder?

Hudson Taylor was a missionary to China in the 19th century and founded China Inland Mission. The following anecdote, recounted by Dr. and Mrs. Howard Taylor, details his devotional habits while ministering in China.

> It was not easy for Mr. Taylor in his changeful life, to make time for prayer and Bible study, but he knew that it was vital. Well do the writers remember traveling with him month after month in northern China, by cart and wheelbarrow with the poorest of inns at night. Often with only one large

> room for coolies and travelers alike, they would screen off a corner for their father and another for themselves, with curtains of some sort; and then, after sleep at last had brought a measure of quiet, they would hear a match struck and see the flicker of candlelight which told that Mr. Taylor, however weary, was poring over the little Bible in two volumes always at hand. From two to four A.M. was the time he usually gave to prayer; the time he could be most sure of being undisturbed to wait upon God.[3]

***QUESTION 8:** How does Hudson Taylor's willingness to lose sleep so that he could spend time poring over the Bible testify to the Bible's majesty? What did the Scriptures offer him that a contemporary work of poetry or biography could not have offered? How have you experienced the unique majesty of Scripture?

DAY 5: THE PURITY OF THE SCRIPTURES

> Question Four: How doth it appear that the Scriptures are the Word of God?
>
> Answer: The Scriptures manifest themselves to be the Word of God,
>
> 1. by their majesty
>
> 2. and purity;

> 3. by the consent of all the parts,
>
> 4. and the scope of the whole, which is to give all glory to God;
>
> 5. by their light and power to convince and convert sinners, to comfort and build up believers unto salvation.
>
> 6. But the Spirit of God, bearing witness by and with the Scriptures in the heart of man, is alone able fully to persuade it that they are the very Word of God.

The second evidence for the Bible's reliability is its purity. To see this attribute of Scripture being described and praised, consider Psalm 12:6, which you studied in a previous lesson.

PSALM 12:6

> 6 *The words of the* LORD *are pure words, like silver refined in a furnace on the ground, purified seven times.*

***QUESTION 9:** What does it mean to say that the Bible is pure? How does the imagery of purified silver help explain this concept? Why do you think David adds that the words of the Lord have been purified "seven times"?

Psalm 19:7–11, another text you have seen before, describes the purity of the Bible. Study this passage and then answer the question below.

PSALM 19:7–11

> 7 *The law of the* LORD *is perfect, reviving the soul; the testimony of the* LORD *is sure, making wise the simple;* 8 *the precepts of the* LORD *are right, rejoicing the heart; the commandment of the* LORD *is pure, enlightening the eyes;* 9 *the fear of the* LORD *is clean, enduring forever; the rules of the* LORD *are true, and righteous altogether.* 10 *More to be desired are they than gold, even much fine gold; sweeter also than honey and drippings of the honeycomb.* 11 *Moreover, by them is your servant warned; in keeping them there is great reward.*

QUESTION 10: Underline the statement, "the commandment of the LORD is pure" (verse 8). What is the connection between this statement and the next: "enlightening the eyes"? How does the purity of Scripture make it more desirable than gold and honey?

> If you have a choice between the Word of God and GOLD, choose the Word of God. If you have a choice between the Word of God and MUCH gold, choose the Word of God. If you have a choice between the Word of God and much FINE gold, choose the Word of God. The point is plain. The benefits of knowing and doing the Word of God are greater than all that money can buy.

> So if you are tempted to read the stock page before you read the Bible in the morning, remind yourself that this is not shrewd behavior. It's like the child who chooses the penny over the dime because it's bigger. Adults look on and shake their heads and try to teach children how to see what is really more valuable. That is no doubt the way the angels in heaven look down at childish businessmen who study the stock page before they study the Bible. There is a difference however: the benefits of the Word of God over the benefits of gold are far greater than ten to one.[4]

FURTHER UP AND FURTHER IN

Read or listen to "Wonderful Things from Your Word," an online sermon at the Desiring God Web site.

QUESTION 11: What kinds of things can you see in the Word without God opening the eyes of your heart?

QUESTION 12: What is it that you cannot see unless God opens the eyes of your heart? Why is seeing this sight so important?

John Piper refers to 2 Corinthians 3:18. Study this verse and answer the following question.

2 CORINTHIANS 3:18

> [18] *And we all, with unveiled face, beholding the glory of the Lord, are being transformed into the same image from one degree of glory to another. For this comes from the Lord who is the Spirit.*

QUESTION 13: According to this text, how are people changed into the likeness of Jesus? What is the connection between this verse and Psalm 119:18?

QUESTION 14: Respond to this statement: "Religious excitement in the presence of miracles is a natural thing and has no necessary spiritual or supernatural dimension. The gifts of the Spirit are precious, but infinitely more important is the eye-opening illumination of the Holy Spirit so that we see the glory of Christ in the Word." Do you agree? Can you think of any examples in the Bible where excitement over miracles was no sure sign of genuine faith?

QUESTION 15: Suppose someone came to you and confessed that they were dissatisfied with their Bible reading and felt dry in their relationship with God. What would you advise this person to do?

WHILE YOU WATCH THE DVD, TAKE NOTES

Why is it not a good idea to take a leap in the dark when you decide to trust the Bible?

How does the message of the Bible vindicate itself? What does it say to the heart of a believer?

Why do we need to continually pray with David, "Open my eyes, that I may behold wondrous things out of your law" (Psalm 119:18)?

The words of the Lord are like words that have been put through a furnace seven times to burn away all the _____________.

How did God vindicate himself to the former Jehovah's Witness who gave her testimony in John Piper's church in Germany?

AFTER YOU WATCH THE DVD, DISCUSS WHAT YOU'VE LEARNED

1) Discuss why the Bible is not honored by an uninformed trust. Do you agree with John Piper's argument? Can you think of other examples where this principle applies?

2) Reflect on seasons or days in your life when you have not beheld wondrous things out of the Bible. Can you identify any factors that contributed to the difficulty? How did God eventually bring you out of those times? If you are currently in a dark season, how might you better strive to see the glory of Christ in the Word more clearly?

3) What role did the majesty of the Scriptures play in your coming to Christ? How do you currently experience this majesty? How would you attempt to explain the divine nature of the Word of God to someone who has never seen it?

AFTER YOU DISCUSS, MAKE APPLICATION

1) What was the most meaningful part of this lesson for you? Was there a sentence, a concept, or an idea that really struck you? Why? Record your thoughts in the space below.

2) Memorize Psalm 119:18 and pray it this week as you come to read the Bible. Record any insights that God reveals to you in the space below.

NOTES

1. John Piper, "Why We Believe the Bible, Part 1," an online resource at the Desiring God Web site.
2. John Piper, "Why We Believe the Bible, Part 1," an online resource at the Desiring God Web site.
3. John Piper, *Desiring God* (Sisters, OR: Multnomah, 2003), 151–52.
4. John Piper, "Sweeter than Honey, Better than Gold," an online sermon at the Desiring God Web site.

LESSON 8

HOW CAN WE JUSTIFY THE CLAIM THAT THE BIBLE IS GOD'S WORD? (PART 2)

A Companion Study to the Why We Believe the Bible DVD, Session 7

LESSON OBJECTIVES

It is our prayer that after you have finished this lesson . . .

- You will be able to articulate the unifying message of the Bible.
- You will desire to embrace and boldly declare the whole counsel of God.
- You will understand how the Bible's emphasis on giving glory to God argues for its reliability.

BEFORE YOU WATCH THE DVD, STUDY AND PREPARE

DAY 1: THE CONSENT OF ALL THEIR PARTS

In the previous lesson you interacted with the first two evidences for the authority of the Bible from the Westminster Larger

Catechism and saw that the Scriptures show themselves to be God's Word by their majesty and their purity. In this lesson you will explore the next two evidences: the Bible is a coherent whole and its aim is to give glory to God.

> Question Four: How doth it appear that the Scriptures are the Word of God?
>
> Answer: The Scriptures manifest themselves to be the Word of God,
>
> 1. by their majesty
>
> 2. and purity;
>
> 3. by the consent of all the parts,
>
> 4. and the scope of the whole, which is to give all glory to God;
>
> 5. by their light and power to convince and convert sinners, to comfort and build up believers unto salvation.
>
> 6. But the Spirit of God, bearing witness by and with the Scriptures in the heart of man, is alone able fully to persuade it that they are the very Word of God.

The Bible teaches that it contains a unified message. To see this, consider Paul's words to the Ephesian elders in the following passage.

ACTS 20:22–27

[22] *And now, behold, I am going to Jerusalem, constrained by*
the Spirit, not knowing what will happen to me there, [23] *except*
that the Holy Spirit testifies to me in every city that imprison-
ment and afflictions await me. [24] *But I do not account my life*
of any value nor as precious to myself, if only I may finish my
course and the ministry that I received from the Lord Jesus, to
testify to the gospel of the grace of God. [25] *And now, behold,*
I know that none of you among whom I have gone about
proclaiming the kingdom will see my face again. [26] *Therefore*
I testify to you this day that I am innocent of the blood of all
of you, [27] *for I did not shrink from declaring to you the whole*
counsel of God.

***QUESTION 1:** What is "the whole counsel of God"? What would have tempted Paul to shrink back from declaring it?

Now compare Acts 20:22–27 with the following passage.

ACTS 18:5–6

[5] *When Silas and Timothy arrived from Macedonia, Paul*
was occupied with the word, testifying to the Jews that the
Christ was Jesus. [6] *And when they opposed and reviled him,*
he shook out his garments and said to them, "Your blood be
on your own heads! I am innocent. From now on I will go to
the Gentiles."

QUESTION 2: In light of this passage, what does Paul mean by "the blood of all of you" in Acts 20:26? How did declaring the whole counsel of God make him innocent of this blood?

DAY 2: ALL THE PROPHETS BEAR WITNESS

Study Acts 10:42–43 and Acts 26:22–23.

ACTS 10:42–43

> [42] *And he [Jesus] commanded us to preach to the people and to testify that he is the one appointed by God to be judge of the living and the dead.* [43] *To him all the prophets bear witness that everyone who believes in him receives forgiveness of sins through his name.*

ACTS 26:22–23

> [22] *To this day I have had the help that comes from God, and so I stand here testifying both to small and great, saying nothing but what the prophets and Moses said would come to pass:*
> [23] *that the Christ must suffer and that, by being the first to rise from the dead, he would proclaim light both to our people and to the Gentiles.*

***QUESTION 3:** According to these verses, what is the unifying message of the prophets and Moses? Why is it significant that they all say the same thing? How is this an argument for the authority of the Bible?

Reflect on the following explanation.

> The Bible makes God out to love his name and his glory with omnipotent energy and unbounded joy. And then it pictures him choosing God-belittling sinners for his court, and rejoicing over the very people who have despised his glory and cheapened his name.
>
> I really don't believe it is possible to grasp the central drama of the Bible until we begin to feel this tension. Until the coming of Jesus Christ, the Bible is like a piece of music whose dissonance begs for some final resolution into harmony. Redemptive history is like a symphony with two great themes: the theme of God's passion to promote his glory; and the theme of God's inscrutable electing love for sinners who have scorned that very glory. Again and again all through the Bible these two great themes carry along the symphony of history. They interweave and interpenetrate, and we know that some awesome Composer is at work here. But for centuries we don't hear the resolution. The harmony always escapes us, and we have to wait.
>
> The death and resurrection of Jesus Christ is the resolution of the symphony of history. In the death of Jesus the two themes of God's love for his glory and his love for sinners are resolved. As in all good symphonies there had been

hints and suggestions of the final resolution. That is what we have in Isaiah 53 seven hundred years before Jesus came.

God's pleasure in his name and his pleasure in doing good to sinners meet and marry in his pleasure in bruising the Son of God.[1]

QUESTION 4: According to this excerpt, what are the two great themes of the symphony of redemptive history? Where do they find resolution? After pondering this and the verses you have already studied, together with any other verses you can think of, what is the unifying message of the Bible? Express this message as it relates to the glory of God.

God is righteous. This means that he recognizes, welcomes, loves, and upholds with infinite jealousy and energy what is infinitely valuable, namely, the worth of God. God's righteous passion and delight is to display and uphold his infinitely valuable glory. This is not a vague theological conjecture. It flows inevitably from dozens of biblical texts that show God in the relentless pursuit of praise and honor from creation to consummation.[2]

DAY 3: THE SCOPE OF THE WHOLE IS TO GIVE GLORY TO GOD

Question Four: How doth it appear that the Scriptures are the Word of God?

Answer: The Scriptures manifest themselves to be the Word of God,

1. by their majesty

2. and purity;

3. by the consent of all the parts,

4. and the scope of the whole, which is to give all glory to God;

5. by their light and power to convince and convert sinners, to comfort and build up believers unto salvation.

6. But the Spirit of God, bearing witness by and with the Scriptures in the heart of man, is alone able fully to persuade it that they are the very Word of God.

The fourth evidence for the Bible's reliability is "the scope of the whole, which is to give all glory to God."

Study Romans 3:19 and Romans 3:27.

ROMANS 3:19

> 19 *Now we know that whatever the law says it speaks to those who are under the law, so that every mouth may be stopped, and the whole world may be held accountable to God.*

ROMANS 3:27

> [27] *Then what becomes of our boasting? It is excluded. By what kind of law? By a law of works? No, but by the law of faith.*

QUESTION 5: What do these texts suggest about the glory of God and the glory of man? Which is exalted? Which is abased? Why is boasting so evil?

***QUESTION 6:** Are you more prone to listen to someone who promotes himself or who points away from himself to God? In light of the texts above, why do you think this is? Do you think this concept could argue for the Bible's reliability? Explain.

DAY 4: THE ONE WHO SPEAKS ON HIS OWN AUTHORITY SEEKS HIS OWN GLORY

Read the following passage to see how Jesus drew attention to his Father.

JOHN 7:16–18

[16] So Jesus answered them, "My teaching is not mine, but his who sent me. [17] If anyone's will is to do God's will, he will know whether the teaching is from God or whether I am speaking on my own authority. [18] The one who speaks on his own authority seeks his own glory; but the one who seeks the glory of him who sent him is true, and in him there is no falsehood."

QUESTION 7: According to Jesus, how can a person know whether or not his teaching is from God? What does this mean?

***QUESTION 8:** How does the fact that Jesus sought the glory of him who sent him authenticate the truth of his message? What might this imply about the whole Bible?

If you ever meet a man who cares nothing for the praise and approval of men (Mark 12:14), but whose one controlling desire is to glorify God whom he loves with all his heart, believe that man. He is true. This is what his brothers should have seen in his miraculous works: not the mere display of power, but the all-consuming love to God which emptied Jesus of the typical human craving for praise and acclaim and approval. He does not speak on his own authority, nor does he seek his own glory (7:18), nor does he do his miracles in his own name: "The works which I do in my Father's name, *these* bear witness concerning me" (John 10:25). The basis of faith in Jesus is not just the raw show of miraculous power, it is the soul of the power, the heart and motive from which it comes. Only the people who saw within the miracles what the man was really like, what made him tick, could truly believe on him. It was the shining out of this inner life that marks Jesus as true: "He who seeks the glory of him who sent him is true." This is the soul of all he did, and this is the true basis of saving faith: Love seeks not its own glory (1 Corinthians 13:5); it is consumed with God's glory. So Jesus lived not for the praise of men, but for their salvation. He had one all-consuming motive—to glorify God through the salvation of men. That is the kind of man you can trust. His character is self-authenticating. It is the basis of a reasonable and saving faith.[3]

DAY 5: I DO NOT RECEIVE GLORY FROM PEOPLE

Study Jesus' words to the Jews in the following passage.

JOHN 5:41–47

> 41 *I do not receive glory from people.* 42 *But I know that you*
> *do not have the love of God within you.* 43 *I have come in*
> *my Father's name, and you do not receive me. If another*
> *comes in his own name, you will receive him.* 44 *How can*
> *you believe, when you receive glory from one another and*
> *do not seek the glory that comes from the only God?* 45 *Do*
> *not think that I will accuse you to the Father. There is one*
> *who accuses you: Moses, on whom you have set your hope.*
> 46 *For if you believed Moses, you would believe me; for he*
> *wrote of me.* 47 *But if you do not believe his writings, how*
> *will you believe my words?*

***QUESTION 9:** Meditate on Jesus' statement that the Jews "receive glory from one another and do not seek the glory that comes from the only God." With this in mind, why do you think the Jews would not receive Jesus who had come in his Father's name but would receive someone who came in his own name?

QUESTION 10: In your own words, summarize why the Bible's giving glory to God is an argument for its authority. Do you find this to be a compelling argument? Why or why not?

FURTHER UP AND FURTHER IN

Read "Biblical Texts to Show God's Zeal for His Own Glory," an online article at the Desiring God Web site.

John Piper writes, "Probably no text in the Bible reveals the passion of God for his own glory more clearly and bluntly as Isaiah 48:9–11 . . . " Study this passage and then answer the following questions.

ISAIAH 48:9–11

> [9] *For my name's sake I defer my anger, for the sake of my praise I restrain it for you, that I may not cut you off.* [10] *Behold, I have refined you, but not as silver; I have tried you in the furnace of affliction.* [11] *For my own sake, for my own sake, I do it, for how should my name be profaned? My glory I will not give to another.*

QUESTION 11: Underline each phrase that refers to God's name, his praise, or some related idea. According to this text, what is God most passionate about? Why is this offensive to many people?

QUESTION 12: What does it mean for God to defer his anger for his name's sake? Why is this good news for us?

Read the following passage.

ISAIAH 43:6–7

> 6 *I will say to the north, Give up, and to the south, Do not with-*
> *hold; bring my sons from afar and my daughters from the end of*
> *the earth,* 7 *everyone who is called by my name, whom I created*
> *for my glory, whom I formed and made.*

QUESTION 13: What does it mean that God created us for his glory? Be as clear and specific as possible.

Examine the following passage.

ROMANS 3:25–26

> 25 *. . . God put [Christ] forward as a propitiation by his blood,*
> *to be received by faith. This was to show God's righteousness,*
> *because in his divine forbearance he had passed over former sins.*
> 26 *It was to show his righteousness at the present time, so that he*
> *might be just and the justifier of the one who has faith in Jesus.*

QUESTION 14: According to this text, why did God send his Son to die for sins? In what way does the cross show God's righteousness?

QUESTION 15: In your own words, summarize the unifying message of the passages in the article noted on page 123. How does this affect the way you think about the Bible?

WHILE YOU WATCH THE DVD, TAKE NOTES

The Bible, as diverse and big as it is, with all of its different authors, is an amazingly ______________ story.

What phrase in Romans 6:17 captures the idea of "the whole counsel of God" in Acts 20:27?

_______________________ is the way you magnify God and ________________ is the way you magnify yourself and your independence.

What message is written all over Jesus' life? Why is this self-authenticating?

Why would the Pharisees have preferred Jesus to come in his own name?

AFTER YOU WATCH THE DVD, DISCUSS WHAT YOU'VE LEARNED

1) What doctrines within the whole counsel of God are you most tempted to shrink back from declaring? Why? Discuss how you can encourage one another to be bolder in these areas.

2) Review how the Bible's emphasis on giving glory to God is an evidence of its reliability. How would you explain this to someone who hates the glory of God?

3) In what ways are you prone to live for your own name? Think of specific examples in your life that demonstrate this. Spend time praying for one another about these areas.

AFTER YOU DISCUSS, MAKE APPLICATION

1) What was the most meaningful part of this lesson for you? Was there a sentence, a concept, or an idea that really struck you? Why? Record your thoughts in the space below.

2) Meditate on John 5:39–47. In what ways do you live to receive glory from other people? Pray for greater desire to seek the glory that comes from the only God. Record your reflections below.

NOTES

1. John Piper, *The Pleasures of God* (Sisters, OR: Multnomah, 2003), 158–59.
2. John Piper, *Let the Nations Be Glad!* (Grand Rapids, MI: Baker, 2003), 22.
3. John Piper, "Jesus Is Precious Because His Biblical Portrait Is True," an online sermon at the Desiring God Web site.

LESSON 9

NATURAL REVELATION AND THE RELIABILITY OF THE BIBLE

A Companion Study to the Why We Believe the Bible DVD, Session 8

LESSON OBJECTIVES

It is our prayer that after you have finished this lesson . . .

- You will better grasp the purpose and the limitations of natural revelation.
- You will understand how natural revelation contributes to the conviction that the Bible is the Word of God.
- You will desire to make use of creation to exult more fully in the glory of God.

BEFORE YOU WATCH THE DVD, STUDY AND PREPARE

DAY 1: THE HEAVENS DECLARE THE GLORY OF GOD

In the last lesson you saw that one of the evidences for the reliability of the Bible is the fact that its scope is to give glory to God.

This raises a question, however. How can a human heart begin to see that God is glorious so that, when it beholds the God-glorifying nature of the Bible, it recognizes a compelling harmony? The purpose of this lesson is to examine the role natural revelation plays in answering that question.

Natural revelation—also called general revelation—refers to what God has revealed about himself through creation. This is contrasted with special revelation, which has to do with what God has revealed about himself through the Bible.

Psalm 19:1–4 provides a helpful statement about natural revelation. Study this passage and then answer the following questions.

PSALM 19:1–4

> [1] *The heavens declare the glory of God, and the sky above proclaims his handiwork.* [2] *Day to day pours out speech, and night to night reveals knowledge.* [3] *There is no speech, nor are there words, whose voice is not heard.* [4] *Their voice goes out through all the earth, and their words to the end of the world.*

***QUESTION 1:** In what way do the heavens declare the glory of God? List several characteristics of God that are revealed through a spectacular sunset or a starry night sky. How have you experienced the glory of God through beholding what he has created?

QUESTION 2: What does it mean that "Their voice goes out through all the earth, and their words to the end of the world"? What is this voice? Who hears this voice?

The message of creation is this: *there is a great God of glory and power and generosity behind all this awesome universe; you belong to him; he is patient with you in sustaining your rebellious life; turn and bank your hope on him and delight yourself in him, not his handiwork.* Day pours forth the "speech" of that message to all that will listen in the day, speaking with blindingly bright sun and blue sky and clouds and untold shapes and colors of all things visible. Night pours forth the "knowledge" of the same message to all who will listen at night, speaking with great dark voids and summer moons and countless stars and strange sounds and cool breezes and northern lights. Day and night are saying one thing: God is glorious! God is glorious! God is glorious![1]

DAY 2: HE DID NOT LEAVE HIMSELF WITHOUT WITNESS

Barnabas and Paul addressed an idolatrous crowd at Lystra in Acts 14:15–17. Read this passage and respond to the following questions.

ACTS 14:15–17

> [15] *Men, why are you doing these things? We also are men, of*
> *like nature with you, and we bring you good news, that you*
> *should turn from these vain things to a living God, who made*
> *the heaven and the earth and the sea and all that is in them.*
> [16] *In past generations he allowed all the nations to walk in their*
> *own ways.* [17] *Yet he did not leave himself without witness, for he*
> *did good by giving you rains from heaven and fruitful seasons,*
> *satisfying your hearts with food and gladness.*

***QUESTION 3:** What is the witness Barnabas and Paul are referring to? According to this passage, what other aspects of the creation testify to the nature of God? What do these things reveal about God?

QUESTION 4: What are the limitations of natural revelation? In other words, what has God revealed about himself in the Bible that is not accessible through only viewing the creation?

DAY 3: THEY ARE WITHOUT EXCUSE

Romans 1:19–21 is a central text for understanding natural revelation. Meditate on this passage before answering the following questions.

ROMANS 1:19–21

> [19] *For what can be known about God is plain to them, because*
> *God has shown it to them.* [20] *For his invisible attributes, namely,*
> *his eternal power and divine nature, have been clearly perceived,*
> *ever since the creation of the world, in the things that have been*
> *made. So they are without excuse.* [21] *For although they knew*
> *God, they did not honor him as God or give thanks to him,*
> *but they became futile in their thinking, and their foolish hearts*
> *were darkened.*

***QUESTION 5:** Trace Paul's logic in these verses. Explain why all men are without excuse. How does this relate to natural revelation?

QUESTION 6: Paul says every person can perceive God's invisible attributes "in the things that have been made." Is this perception enough for salvation? Why or why not? Explain your answer with reference to this passage and the broader context of Romans.

DAY 4: THE MESSAGE OF CREATION

***QUESTION 7:** Imagine you had no access to the Bible and all you had available to you was everything you could see in the world around you. Assuming there was a Being who had caused all that you see, what might you conclude about his nature and your relationship to him?

Compare your answers to the following list of suggestions.

My existence in the world confronts me as soon as I am conscious of it with:

› A Single Originator of all that is.

› One who is totally self-sufficient with no dependence on anything outside himself to be all that he is.

› One without beginning or ending or progress from worse to better, and therefore absolute and perfect.

› One on whom I am dependent moment by moment for all things, none of which I deserve, and who is therefore beneficent.

› One who is Personal and accounts for transcendent personhood in human beings.

- One who accounts for the intelligent design manifest in the macro (galaxies) and micro (molecules and cells) universe.

- One who knows all.

- One who deserves to be reverenced and admired and looked to for guidance and help.

- One who sees me as guilty for failure in not rendering him what he deserves, and who thus gives ultimate explanation to universal bad conscience.

- One who might save me, but would need to do it in a way that overcomes my evil impulse to resist him, and would have to make a way for his honor to be sustained while not punishing me for treason.[2]

QUESTION 8: How did your answers compare with the list above? Were there any suggestions you had that were not on the list, or vice versa? Are there any points on the list with which you disagree? Why or why not?

DAY 5: BRINGING IT BACK TO THE BIBLE

***QUESTION 9:** Review your notes from the previous lesson. What does the Westminster Larger Catechism mean when it says that an evidence for the authority of the Bible is "the scope of the whole, which is to give all glory to God"? How does this argue for the truth of the Scriptures?

QUESTION 10: Relate your answer to the previous question to the content of this lesson. How does natural revelation serve the conviction that the Bible is true?

FURTHER UP AND FURTHER IN

Read or listen to "Do You See the Joy of God in the Sun?" an online sermon at the Desiring God Web site.

QUESTION 11: John Piper divides Psalm 19 into two sections: verses 1–6 and verses 7–11. What "ministry" does each section describe? What are the differences between these two ministries?

QUESTION 12: How does viewing God's creation minister humility to those who will receive it?

QUESTION 13: David writes in Psalm 19:1, "The heavens declare the glory of God, and the sky above proclaims his handiwork." How would you argue that other aspects of the creation declare the glory of God, as well? Can you think of any biblical texts that would support this?

QUESTION 14: Describe the analogy of viewing a painting. What two things are immediately suggested to our minds when viewing someone else's work of art? Do you find this to be true when you look at the heavens? Explain.

QUESTION 15: Why is it good news that the glory of God is a happy thing? How is this happiness displayed in the creation?

WHILE YOU WATCH THE DVD, TAKE NOTES

Get into astronomy, get into biology, get into chemistry, get into physics, and ______________!

How did Professor Goppelt respond when John Piper asked him why he believed in Jesus?

Is it ever appropriate to try to be a skeptic about God's existence? Why or why not?

What is process theology?

Where does a bad conscience come from?

AFTER YOU WATCH THE DVD, DISCUSS WHAT YOU'VE LEARNED

1) How can an unbeliever be condemned if he or she has never heard the gospel? Discuss how this relates to natural revelation.

2) Describe a time in your life when experiencing some aspect of the creation awoke wonder and worship in your heart. Were you reading about it or viewing it with your own eyes? What was it about what you were witnessing that caused this response? What did it reveal about the nature of God?

3) What types of injustices make you feel morally outraged? How does this emotional reaction argue for the existence of God?

AFTER YOU DISCUSS, MAKE APPLICATION

1) What was the most meaningful part of this lesson for you? Was there a sentence, a concept, or an idea that really struck you? Why? Record your thoughts in the space below.

2) If you are able, go outside this week and intentionally observe some facet of the wonder of creation. Enjoy a sunset, or maybe an anthill. How do the eyes of your heart see the glory of God in these things? Record your observations below.

NOTES

1. John Piper, *The Pleasures of God*, 86.
2. John Piper, "Why We Believe the Bible, Part 1," an online resource at the Desiring God Web site.

LESSON 10

THE INTERNAL TESTIMONY OF THE HOLY SPIRIT

A Companion Study to the Why We Believe the Bible DVD, Session 9

LESSON OBJECTIVES

It is our prayer that after you have finished this lesson . . .

- You will revel in the power of the Scriptures to awaken and sustain faith.
- You will be able to explain the nature and function of the internal testimony of the Holy Spirit.
- You will feel better equipped to give a simple and profound defense for your belief in the gospel.

BEFORE YOU WATCH THE DVD, STUDY AND PREPARE

DAY 1: THE LIGHT OF THE GOSPEL

In this lesson you will interact with the remainder of the Westminster Larger Catechism's explanation of how the Bible demonstrates itself to be the Word of God. Ultimately, the Catechism urges the necessity of what some have called "the internal testimony of the Holy Spirit." It is this testimony that finally convinces a person that the Bible is the Word of God. What is this testimony? How does it operate in the soul? This lesson intends to help you answer these questions.

Before considering the internal testimony of the Holy Spirit, however, there remains one final evidence for the reliability of the Scriptures.

Question Four: How doth it appear that the Scriptures are the Word of God?

Answer: The Scriptures manifest themselves to be the Word of God,

1. by their majesty

2. and purity;

3. by the consent of all the parts,

4. and the scope of the whole, which is to give all glory to God;

5. by their light and power to convince and convert sinners, to comfort and build up believers unto salvation.

6. But the Spirit of God, bearing witness by and with the Scriptures in the heart of man, is alone able fully to persuade it that they are the very Word of God.

Study the following passage.

2 CORINTHIANS 4:4–6

> [4] *In their case the god of this world has blinded the minds of the unbelievers, to keep them from seeing the light of the gospel of the glory of Christ, who is the image of God.* [5] *For what we proclaim is not ourselves, but Jesus Christ as Lord, with ourselves as your servants for Jesus' sake.* [6] *For God, who said, "Let light shine out of darkness," has shone in our hearts to give the light of the knowledge of the glory of God in the face of Jesus Christ.*

QUESTION 1: How does this passage describe conversion? What is the state of the unbeliever before salvation? What happens to change this state?

***QUESTION 2:** What does Paul mean by "the light of the gospel of the glory of Christ, who is the image of God" and the "light of the knowledge of the glory of God in the face of Jesus Christ"? Are these the same light? What does it look like to "see" this light?

DAY 2: THE BIBLE AND THE NEW BIRTH

Read Acts 20:32; James 1:18; and 1 Peter 1:22–2:3.

ACTS 20:32

[32] And now I commend you to God and to the word of his grace, which is able to build you up and to give you the inheritance among all those who are sanctified.

JAMES 1:18

[18] Of his own will he brought us forth by the word of truth, that we should be a kind of firstfruits of his creatures.

1 PETER 1:22–2:3

[22] Having purified your souls by your obedience to the truth for
a sincere brotherly love, love one another earnestly from a pure
heart, [23] since you have been born again, not of perishable seed
but of imperishable, through the living and abiding word of
God; [24] for "All flesh is like grass and all its glory like the flower
of grass. The grass withers, and the flower falls, [25] but the word
of the Lord remains forever." And this word is the good news
that was preached to you. [1] So put away all malice and all deceit
and hypocrisy and envy and all slander. [2] Like newborn infants,
long for the pure spiritual milk, that by it you may grow up into
salvation— [3] if indeed you have tasted that the Lord is good.

***QUESTION 3:** What role does the Word of God have in the new birth and in strengthening the faith of believers? How does this argue for the authority of the Scriptures?

Interact with the following account of St. Augustine's conversion.

> I flung myself down beneath a fig tree and gave way to the tears which now streamed from my eyes. . . . In my misery I kept crying, "How long shall I go on saying 'tomorrow, tomorrow'? Why not now? Why not make an end of my ugly sins at this moment?" . . . All at once I heard the singsong voice of a child in a nearby house. Whether it was the voice of a boy or a girl I cannot say, but again and again it repeated the refrain "Take it and read, take it and read." At this I looked up, thinking hard whether there was any kind of game in which children used to chant words like these, but I could not remember ever hearing them before. I stemmed my flood of tears and stood up, telling myself that this could only be a divine command to open my book of Scripture and read the first passage on which my eyes should fall.
>
> So I hurried back to the place where Alypius was sitting . . . seized [the book of Paul's epistles] and opened it, and in silence I read the first passage on which my eyes fell: "Not in reveling in drunkenness, not in lust and wantonness, not in quarrels and rivalries. Rather, arm yourselves with the Lord Jesus Christ; spend no more thought on nature and nature's appetites" (Romans 13:13–14). I had no wish to read more and no need to do so. For in an instant, as I came to the end of the sentence, it was as though the light of confidence flooded into my heart and all the darkness of doubt was dispelled.[1]

QUESTION 4: Explain Augustine's conversion with reference to the texts you have studied so far in this lesson. How is the Bible's "light and power to convince and convert sinners" evident in this account?

DAY 3: JOHN CALVIN AND THE INTERNAL TESTIMONY OF THE HOLY SPIRIT

The final answer of the Westminster Larger Catechism provides the bedrock of our confidence that the Bible is the Word of God.

> Question Four: How doth it appear that the Scriptures are the Word of God?
>
> Answer: The Scriptures manifest themselves to be the Word of God,
>
> 1. by their majesty
>
> 2. and purity;
>
> 3. by the consent of all the parts,
>
> 4. and the scope of the whole, which is to give all glory to God;

> 5. by their light and power to convince and convert sinners, to comfort and build up believers unto salvation.
>
> 6. But the Spirit of God, bearing witness by and with the Scriptures in the heart of man, is alone able fully to persuade it that they are the very Word of God.

Ponder John Calvin's explanation of how the Holy Spirit bears witness to the authority of the Scriptures.

> A most pernicious error widely prevails that Scripture has only so much weight as is conceded to it by the consent of the church. As if the eternal and inviolable truth of God depended upon the decision of men! . . . Yet, if this is so, what will happen to miserable consciences seeking firm assurance of eternal life if all promises of it consist in and depend solely upon the judgment of men? (*Institutes*, I, vii, 1)[2]

QUESTION 5: What danger is Calvin confronting? If the decision of men is not the final argument for the authority of the Bible, what is?

Calvin continues by explaining what he means by the "testimony of the Spirit."

> The testimony of the Spirit is more excellent than all reason. For as God alone is a fit witness of himself in his Word, the Word will not find acceptance in men's hearts before it is sealed by the inward testimony of the Spirit. The same Spirit therefore who has spoken through the mouths of the prophets must penetrate into our hearts to persuade us that they faithfully proclaimed what had been divinely commanded . . . because until he illumines their minds, they ever waver among many doubts! (*Institutes*, I, vii, 4)
>
> Therefore illumined by his [the Holy Spirit's] power, we believe neither by our own nor by anyone else's judgment that Scripture is from God; but above human judgment we affirm with utter certainty (just as if we were gazing upon the majesty of God himself) that it has flowed to us from the very mouth of God by the ministry of men. (*Institutes*, I, vii, 5)[3]

***QUESTION 6:** In your own words, how would you explain the testimony of the Spirit? How does this testimony convince us that the Bible is from God? Why is it essential that God himself bear witness to his own Word?

DAY 4: THE BIBLE IS SELF-AUTHENTICATING

J. I. Packer attempts to describe John Calvin's treatment of the internal witness of the Holy Spirit in the following paragraph. Read his description and then answer the following questions.

> Calvin affirms Scripture to be self-authenticating through the inner witness of the Holy Spirit. What is this "inner witness"? Not a special quality of experience, nor a new, private revelation, nor an existential "decision", but a work of enlightenment whereby, through the medium of verbal testimony, the blind eyes of the spirit are opened, and divine realities come to be recognized and embraced for what they are. This recognition, Calvin says, is as immediate and unanalysable as the perceiving of a color, or a taste, by physical sense—an event about which no more can be said than that when appropriate stimuli were present it happened, and when it happened we know it had happened.[4]

***QUESTION 7:** Packer argues that the inner witness of the Holy Spirit is not a "new, private revelation" but rather is a "work of enlightenment" that happens "through the medium of verbal testimony." How does this agree with the Catechism's answer that the Spirit of God bears witness "by and with the Scriptures in the heart of man"? In light of this, what would you direct someone to read who wants to know if the Bible is the Word of God?

QUESTION 8: Suppose you had a blind friend. How would you explain to him your confidence that the sun is shining as you speak? Ultimately, what would need to happen for your friend to agree that this is true? How does this relate to the internal testimony of the Holy Spirit?

DAY 5: MY SHEEP HEAR MY VOICE

Study the following passage.

JOHN 10:25–28

> 25 *Jesus answered them, "I told you, and you do not believe.*
> *The works that I do in my Father's name bear witness about me,*
> 26 *but you do not believe because you are not part of my flock.*
> 27 *My sheep hear my voice, and I know them, and they follow*
> *me.* 28 *I give them eternal life, and they will never perish, and no*
> *one will snatch them out of my hand."*

QUESTION 9: Why do the sheep in this passage follow Jesus? How do they know it is Jesus' voice that they hear? What must happen for them to recognize his voice?

First John 5:6–11 probably contains the clearest teaching about the internal witness of the Holy Spirit. Read this passage and then answer the following question.

1 JOHN 5:6–11

> [6] *This is he who came by water and blood—Jesus Christ; not by*
> *the water only but by the water and the blood. And the Spirit is*
> *the one who testifies, because the Spirit is the truth.* [7] *For there*
> *are three that testify:* [8] *the Spirit and the water and the blood;*
> *and these three agree.* [9] *If we receive the testimony of men, the*
> *testimony of God is greater, for this is the testimony of God*
> *that he has borne concerning his Son.* [10] *Whoever believes in*
> *the Son of God has the testimony in himself. Whoever does not*
> *believe God has made him a liar, because he has not believed in*
> *the testimony that God has borne concerning his Son.* [11] *And*
> *this is the testimony, that God gave us eternal life, and this life*
> *is in his Son.*

***QUESTION 10:** Why is the testimony of God greater than the testimony of men in this passage? What is the testimony of God? How does this testimony bear witness to the reliability of Jesus?

In other words, "the testimony of God," that is, the inward witness of the Spirit, is greater than any human witness—including, I think the apostle would say in this context, the witness of our own judgment. And what is that testimony of God? It is not merely a word delivered to our judgment for reflection, for then our conviction would rely on our own reflection. What is it then? Verse 11 is the key: "This is the testimony, that God gave us eternal life." I take that to mean that God testifies to us of his reality and the reality of his Son and of the gospel by giving us life from the dead, so that we come alive to his self-authenticating glory in the gospel. In that instant we do not reason from premises to conclusions; rather we see that we are awake, and there is not even a prior human judgment about it to lean on. When Lazarus wakened in the tomb by the call or the "testimony" of Christ, he knew without reasoning that he was alive and that this call awakened him.[5]

FURTHER UP AND FURTHER IN

Read or listen to "A Divine and Supernatural Light Immediately Imparted to the Soul by the Spirit of God: The Unrivaled Legacy of Jonathan Edwards," an online conference message at the Desiring God Web site.

John Piper interacts with 2 Corinthians 4:4–6 in this message. Use this passage as a reference for the following questions.

2 CORINTHIANS 4:4–6

> [4] *In their case the god of this world has blinded the minds of*
> *the unbelievers, to keep them from seeing the light of the gospel*
> *of the glory of Christ, who is the image of God.* [5] *For what*
> *we proclaim is not ourselves, but Jesus Christ as Lord, with*
> *ourselves as your servants for Jesus' sake.* [6] *For God, who said,*
> *"Let light shine out of darkness," has shone in our hearts to*
> *give the light of the knowledge of the glory of God in the face*
> *of Jesus Christ.*

QUESTION 11: What are the three levels of salvation in this passage? Underline the phrase that corresponds to each level and briefly describe what each means.

QUESTION 12: Where is the glory of Christ revealed most clearly? How is this glory self-authenticating?

QUESTION 13: What is the double truth of the gospel? Why are both of these truths essential for our salvation?

QUESTION 14: How does Jonathan Edwards define regeneration? Do you find the imagery of taste or sense to be helpful to you in understanding what the new birth entails? According to this definition, is it enough to affirm certain truths about Jesus to be saved, or must there also be an accompanying delight in who he is?

QUESTION 15: What is the ultimate goal of God in creation? How do the cross of Christ, the imputation of righteousness, and the new birth serve this great goal?

WHILE YOU WATCH THE DVD, TAKE NOTES

Why is the self-authenticating nature of the gospel not irrational?

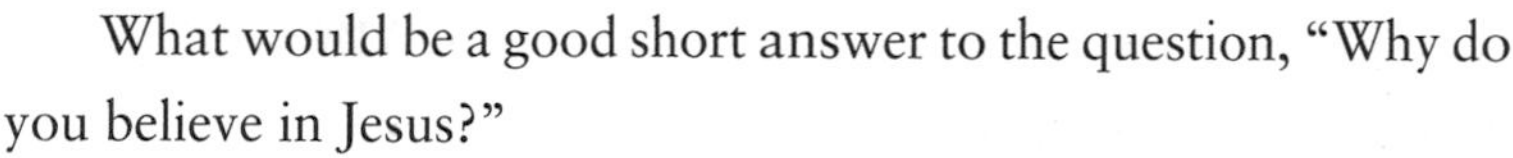

What would be a good short answer to the question, "Why do you believe in Jesus?"

The testimony of the Holy Spirit, he's going to argue, is not ______________ information about the Bible.

When Calvin says, "Hence, it is not right to subject it [Scripture] to proof and reasoning," does he mean that proof and reasoning have no value in arguing for the truth of the Bible? What then does he mean?

Why is it dangerous to look for an extra message from the Holy Spirit telling you to believe the Bible?

AFTER YOU WATCH THE DVD, DISCUSS WHAT YOU'VE LEARNED

1) Discuss the self-authenticating light of the gospel. Is it a circular argument to say that something can be its own evidence? Why or why not?

2) What exactly is the internal witness of the Holy Spirit? Try to define it as clearly and concisely as possible. Are there any questions you still have about this teaching?

3) What have been some significant challenges to your faith? How has seeing the "light of the gospel of the glory of Christ" (2 Corinthians 4:4) enabled you to persevere?

AFTER YOU DISCUSS, MAKE APPLICATION

1) What was the most meaningful part of this lesson for you? Was there a sentence, a concept, or an idea that really struck you? Why? Record your thoughts in the space below.

2) Memorize 2 Corinthians 4:4–6 this week. How does this passage help you understand your own experience of the gospel and of the Bible's authority? Record your reflections below.

NOTES

1. John Piper, "The Swan Is Not Silent: Sovereign Joy in the Life and Thought of St. Augustine," an online conference message at the Desiring God Web site.
2. John Piper, "Why We Believe the Bible, Part 1," an online resource at the Desiring God Web site.
3. John Piper, "Why We Believe the Bible, Part 1," an online resource at the Desiring God Web site.
4. John Piper, *God Is the Gospel* (Wheaton, IL: Crossway, 2005), 81.
5. John Piper, *God Is the Gospel*, 80.

LESSON 11

WHAT DOES IT MEAN THAT THE BIBLE IS INERRANT?

A Companion Study to the Why We Believe the Bible DVD, Session 10

LESSON OBJECTIVES

It is our prayer that after you have finished this lesson . . .

- You will better comprehend the meaning of the inerrancy of Scripture.
- You will be more familiar with common objections to the Bible's truthfulness and how to respond.
- You will love the Word of God more deeply and desire to immerse yourself in it daily.

BEFORE YOU WATCH THE DVD, STUDY AND PREPARE

DAY 1: THE DOCTRINE OF INERRANCY

The BBC Elder Affirmation of Faith states, "We believe that the Bible, consisting of the sixty-six books of the Old and New Testaments, is the infallible Word of God, verbally inspired by

God, and without error in the original manuscripts."[1] The purpose of this lesson is to probe the meaning of the phrase "without error." Most people refer to this attribute of Scripture as the doctrine of inerrancy. Though many within evangelical circles would affirm that the Bible is without error, it is necessary to clarify *in what sense* this is so. For example, can we trust the historical details of Scripture? Is there a place for metaphorical language? What degree of scientific precision should we expect? These are important questions, and this lesson intends to help you come to more settled conclusions about the reliability of the Word of God.

QUESTION 1: How would you define the inerrancy of the Bible?

***QUESTION 2:** What are the dangers of rejecting the inerrancy of Scripture? What if a person says there are only some errors in the Bible?

DAY 2: DEFINING THE TERMS

Respond to the following definition of inerrancy.

The Bible is "without error" in the sense that all that the biblical authors intended to teach is true and does not conflict with reality or with the will of God.[2]

QUESTION 3: How does this definition compare with the definition you provided yesterday? Is there anything you would add or subtract? If so, why?

The following excerpt seeks to explain the significance of the phrase "intended to teach" in the definition given above.

" . . . intended to teach . . . "

I use this phrase for two reasons:

1) A writer should not be accused of error because someone construes their words in a way the writer does not "intend." The meaning of a text is not whatever anyone can construe from the words, but what the writer intends for the language to teach. For example, if I say to a friend in Detroit, "I'll be there at 10 A.M.," meaning Eastern Standard Time; and he construes the words to mean 10 A.M. Central Standard Time, I have not erred if I arrive an hour earlier than he expects. I may have been unclear, but I was not wrong. So the meaning of a writer should not be considered false just because the words could be used to express error.

> 2) The word "teach" reinforces this point by implying that a writer might say things which he is not teaching. For example, I may say to my son, "Pick your mother up at the town square." My teaching is that he should get his mother at the place known as the "town square." I am not teaching that he should lift her off the ground in his arms, nor am I teaching that the town square is the same length on all four sides. If the "town square" is 100' by 105' I have not erred, and if my son never touches his mother, but brings her home from there, he has not disobeyed. Both the word "intended" and the word "teach" are meant to protect a writer from accusation of error when there is none.[3]

***QUESTION 4:** Why is the emphasis on the writer's intention so important? Can you think of an example in your life where someone construed your words to mean something you didn't intend for them to mean? How did that make you feel? How do the clarifications provided above help you understand what the inerrancy of Scripture does and does not mean?

DAY 3: THE SUN STOOD STILL

For the remainder of the lesson, you will interact with various biblical texts which some may regard as problematic in defending the Bible's inerrancy. To begin, consider the following passage.

JOSHUA 10:12–13

12 At that time Joshua spoke to the LORD in the day when the
LORD gave the Amorites over to the sons of Israel, and he said
in the sight of Israel, "Sun, stand still at Gibeon, and moon, in
the Valley of Aijalon." 13 And the sun stood still, and the moon
stopped, until the nation took vengeance on their enemies. Is this
not written in the Book of Jashar? The sun stopped in the midst
of heaven and did not hurry to set for about a whole day.

***QUESTION 5:** Is it accurate for the author to say, "And the sun stood still"? Should he not have rather said, "And the earth ceased rotating, giving the impression that the sun was standing still in the sky?" Can you think of other examples where we describe natural phenomena from our own perspective?

Read the following passage.

REVELATION 6:12–13

12 When he opened the sixth seal, I looked, and behold, there
was a great earthquake, and the sun became black as sackcloth,
the full moon became like blood, 13 and the stars of the sky fell
to the earth as the fig tree sheds its winter fruit when shaken
by a gale.

QUESTION 6: Generally speaking, how big is a star? Could a body with that much mass really fall to the earth? Is John teaching scientific error, or might there be a legitimate meteorological event that would give the appearance of stars falling to the earth?

DAY 4: MULTIPLIED LIKE THE SAND ON THE SEASHORE

Analyze Genesis 22:17–18 and Jeremiah 33:22.

GENESIS 22:17–18

> [17] *I will surely bless you, and I will surely multiply your offspring as the stars of heaven and as the sand that is on the seashore. And your offspring shall possess the gate of his enemies,* [18] *and in your offspring shall all the nations of the earth be blessed, because you have obeyed my voice.*

JEREMIAH 33:22

> [22] *As the host of heaven cannot be numbered and the sands of the sea cannot be measured, so I will multiply the offspring of David my servant, and the Levitical priests who minister to me.*

***QUESTION 7:** In Genesis 22:17, is God intending to say that there will be a one-to-one correspondence between the number of grains of sand on the seashore and the number of Abraham's offspring, or are the grains of sand being used symbolically to represent a countless multitude? How does Jeremiah 33:22 help you decide?

Study the following passage.

REVELATION 20:7–8

> [7] *And when the thousand years are ended, Satan will be released*
> *from his prison* [8] *and will come out to deceive the nations that*
> *are at the four corners of the earth, Gog and Magog, to gather them for battle; their number is like the sand of the sea.*

QUESTION 8: Are there really four corners of the earth? Is that what John is intending to teach? Why or why not? Can you think of any other metaphorical descriptions of nature?

DAY 5: WOMAN, I DO NOT KNOW HIM

Read the following passage.

LUKE 22:56–60

> [56] *Then a servant girl, seeing him as he sat in the light and looking closely at him, said, "This man also was with him."* [57] *But*

he denied it, saying, "Woman, I do not know him." [58] *And a little later someone else saw him and said, "You also are one of them." But Peter said, "Man, I am not."* [59] *And after an interval of about an hour still another insisted, saying, "Certainly this man also was with him, for he too is a Galilean."* [60] *But Peter said, "Man, I do not know what you are talking about." And immediately, while he was still speaking, the rooster crowed.*

QUESTION 9: Was Peter telling the truth when he denied that he knew Jesus? How, then, can the Bible contain false statements such as this and still be without error?

***QUESTION 10:** What other arguments have you heard that attempt to prove that the Bible contains errors? How would you respond to these arguments? How does it comfort you to know that the Bible can be trusted in everything it says?

From everything we have seen it is clear that the Bible is a uniquely glorious book, breathed out by a uniquely glorious God. John Piper has expressed his thanksgiving for this book in an article entitled, "10 Reasons Why I Am Thankful for the God-Breathed Bible." As you read these reasons, may your heart rejoice with gratitude that God has given us his reliable, life-giving Word!

1. The Bible awakens faith, the source of all obedience.

So faith comes from *hearing*, and hearing by *the word of Christ*. (Romans 10:17, NASB)

2. The Bible frees from sin.

You will know the *truth*, and the *truth* will make you free. (John 8:32, NASB)

3. The Bible frees from Satan.

The Lord's bond-servant must not be quarrelsome, but be kind to all, *able to teach*, patient when wronged, with gentleness correcting those who are in opposition, if perhaps God may grant them repentance leading to *the knowledge of the truth*, and they may come to their senses and escape from the snare of the devil, having been held captive by him to do his will. (2 Timothy 2:24–26, NASB)

4. The Bible sanctifies.

Sanctify them in the *truth*; Your word is truth. (John 17:17, NASB)

5. The Bible frees from corruption and empowers godliness.

His divine power has granted to us everything pertaining to life and godliness, through the *true knowledge* of Him who called us by His own glory and excellence. For by these He has granted to us His precious and magnificent *promises*, so that *by them* you may become partakers of *the* divine nature, having escaped the corruption that is in the world by lust. (2 Peter 1:3–4, NASB)

6. The Bible serves love.

And this I pray, that your love may abound still more and more in real *knowledge* and all discernment. (Philippians 1:9, NASB)

But the goal of our *instruction* is love from a pure heart and a good conscience and a sincere faith. (1 Timothy 1:5, NASB)

7. The Bible saves.

Pay close attention to yourself and to *your teaching*; persevere in these things, for as you do this you will ensure salvation both for yourself and for those who hear you. (1 Timothy 4:16, NASB)

Therefore, I testify to you this day that I am innocent of the blood of all men. For I did not shrink from declaring to you *the whole purpose of God.* (Acts 20:26, NASB)

[They will] perish, because they did not receive the love of the *truth* so as to be saved. (2 Thessalonians 2:10, NASB)

8. The Bible gives joy.

These things I have *spoken* to you, that my joy may be in you, and that your joy may be full. (John 15:11, NASB)

9. The Bible reveals the Lord.

And the Lord appeared again at Shiloh, for the Lord revealed himself to Samuel at Shiloh by the word of the Lord. (1 Samuel 3:21, NASB)

10. Therefore, the Bible is the foundation of my happy home and life and ministry and hope of eternity with God.[4]

FURTHER UP AND FURTHER IN

Read or listen to "I Will Meditate on All Your Work and Muse on Your Deeds," an online sermon at the Desiring God Web site.

It would be fitting to conclude our study on the trustworthiness of Scripture with an exhortation to meditate on the Bible in our daily lives. Use this sermon and the following questions to help you pursue God more intentionally through his Word.

QUESTION 11: How should we read the Psalms now that Christ has come?

QUESTION 12: What is the danger of neglecting the Word of God in our daily lives? What will be the result of intentionally reading it, memorizing it, meditating on it, and savoring it?

QUESTION 13: What is the relationship between the Bible and prayer? In other words, how should we read the Bible authentically?

QUESTION 14: How did Asaph in Psalm 77 transition from the discouragement in verses 7–10 to the worship in verses 13–20? What does this remembering, meditating, and musing look like in practice?

QUESTION 15: Spend some time reflecting on the three questions John Piper provides for helping you determine when, where, and how you will read your Bible. How do you plan to live on the Word of God?

WHILE YOU WATCH THE DVD, TAKE NOTES

What answer does John Piper give to the question, "What is the witness of the Spirit in your life that the Son of God is who he says he is?"

What was the name of the popular book in John Piper's college days that attempted to discredit the crucifixion?

By its very nature, liberalism is _______________.

What is one example of an idiomatic exaggeration in our language?

List the key words for each of the ways we should handle the Bible:

1.	5.
2.	6.
3.	7.
4.	8.

AFTER YOU WATCH THE DVD, DISCUSS WHAT YOU'VE LEARNED

1) Have there been any books, television specials, or movies that have threatened your confidence in the Bible? How did you initially respond? Were there any resources that were helpful to you?

2) What objections have you heard to the inerrancy of Scripture? Are there any doubts you still have about this issue? Discuss any remaining questions.

3) Recall the list John Piper provided of ways to handle the Bible. In which areas have you seen the most progress in your life? Where are you the weakest? Spend time praying as a group that God would help you reflect the worth of his Word in your lives.

AFTER YOU DISCUSS, MAKE APPLICATION

1) What was the most meaningful part of this lesson for you? Was there a sentence, a concept, or an idea that really struck you? Why? Record your thoughts in the space below.

2) Get together with a friend this week (preferably a non-believer) and explain to him or her something you have learned from your study of the Bible's trustworthiness. Record your friend's response and any reflections you have below.

NOTES

1. The Bethlehem Baptist Church Elder Affirmation of Faith with Scripture proofs can be accessed at http://hopeingod.org/resources/images/1230.pdf.
2. John Piper, "Why We Believe the Bible, Part 1," an online resource at the Desiring God Web site.
3. John Piper, "Why We Believe the Bible, Part 1," an online resource at the Desiring God Web site.
4. John Piper, "10 Reasons Why I Am Thankful for the God-Breathed Bible," an online article at the Desiring God Web site.

LESSON 12

REVIEW AND CONCLUSION

LESSON OBJECTIVES

It is our prayer that after you have finished this lesson . . .

- You will be able to summarize and synthesize what you've learned.
- You will hear what others in your group have learned.
- You will share with others how you have come to trust in the reliability of Scripture.

WHAT HAVE YOU LEARNED?

There are no study questions to answer in preparation for this lesson. Instead, spend your time writing a few paragraphs that explain what you've learned in this group study. To help you do this, you may choose to review the notes you've taken in the previous lessons. Then, after you've written down what you've learned, write down some questions that still remain in your mind about anything addressed in these lessons. Be prepared to share these reflections and questions with the group in the next lesson.

NOTES

Use this space to record anything in the group discussion that you want to remember.

LEADER'S GUIDE

AS THE LEADER OF THIS GROUP STUDY, it is imperative that you are completely familiar with this study guide and the *Why We Believe the Bible* DVD set. Therefore, it is our strong recommendation that you (1) read and understand the introduction, (2) skim each lesson, surveying its layout and content, and (3) read the entire Leader's Guide *before* you begin the group study and distribute the study guides.

BEFORE LESSON 1

Before the first lesson, you will need to know approximately how many participants you will have in your group study. *Each participant will need his or her own study guide!* Therefore, be sure to order enough study guides. You will distribute these study guides at the beginning of the first lesson.

It is also our strong recommendation that you, as the leader, familiarize yourself with this study guide and the *Why We Believe the Bible* DVD set in order to answer any questions that might arise and also to ensure that each group session runs smoothly and maximizes the learning of the participants. It is not necessary for you to preview *Why We Believe the Bible* in its entirety—although it certainly wouldn't hurt!—but you should be prepared to navigate your way through each DVD menu.

DURING LESSON 1

Each lesson is designed for a one-hour group session. Lessons 2–12 require preparatory work from the participant before this group session. Lesson 1, however, requires no preparation on the part of the participant.

The following schedule is how we suggest that you use the first hour of your group study:

INTRODUCTION TO THE STUDY GUIDE (10 MINUTES)

Introduce this study guide and the *Why We Believe the Bible* DVD. Share with the group why you chose to lead the group study using these resources. Inform your group of the commitment that this study will require and motivate them to work hard. Pray for the twelve-week study, asking God for the grace you will need. Then distribute one study guide to each participant. You may read the Introduction aloud, if you want, or you may immediately turn the group to Lesson 1 (starting on page 11 of this study guide).

PERSONAL INTRODUCTIONS (15 MINUTES)

Since group discussion will be an integral part of this guided study, it is crucial that each participant feels welcome and safe. The goal of each lesson is for every participant to contribute to the discussion in some way. Therefore, during these 15 minutes, have participants introduce themselves. You may choose to use the questions listed in the section entitled, "About Yourself," or you may ask questions of your own choosing.

DISCUSSION (25 MINUTES)

Transition from the time of introductions to the discussion questions, listed under the heading "A Preview of *Why We Believe the Bible*." Invite everyone in the class to respond to these questions, but don't let the discussion become too involved. These questions are designed to spark interest and generate questions. The aim is not to come to definitive answers yet.

REVIEW AND CLOSING (10 MINUTES)

End the group session by reviewing Lesson 2 with the group participants and informing them of the preparation that they must do before the group meets again. Encourage them to be faithful in preparing for the next lesson. Answer any questions that the group may have and then close in prayer.

BEFORE LESSONS 2–11

As the group leader, you should do all the preparation for each lesson that is required of the group participants, that is, the ten study questions. Furthermore, it is highly recommended that you complete the entire "Further Up and Further In" section. This is not required of the group participants, but it will enrich your preparation and help you to guide and shape the conversation more effectively.

The group leader should also preview the session of *Why We Believe the Bible* that will be covered in the next lesson. So, for example, if the group participants are doing the preparatory work for Lesson 3, you should preview *Why We Believe the Bible*, Session 2 before the group meets and views it. Previewing each session will better equip you to understand the material and answer questions. If you want to pause the DVD in the midst of the session in order to clarify or discuss, previewing the session will allow you to plan where you want to take your pauses.

Finally, you may want to supplement or modify the discussion questions or the application assignment. Please remember that *this study guide is a resource*; any additions or changes you make that better match the study to your particular group are encouraged. As the group leader, your own discernment, creativity, and guidance are invaluable, and you should adapt the material as you see fit.

Plan for about two hours of your own preparation before each lesson!

DURING LESSONS 2–11

Again, let us stress that during Lessons 2–11, you may use the group time in whatever way you desire. The following schedule, however, is what we suggest:

DISCUSSION (10 MINUTES)

Begin your time with prayer. The tone you set in your prayer will likely be impressed upon the group participants: if your prayer is serious and heart-felt, the group participants will be serious about prayer; if your prayer is hasty, sloppy, or a token gesture, the group participants will share this same attitude toward prayer. So model the kind of praying that you desire your students to imitate. Remember, the blood of Jesus has bought your access to the throne of grace.

After praying, review the preparatory work that the participants completed. How did they answer the questions? Which questions did they find to be the most interesting or the most confusing? What observations or insights can they share with the group? If you would like to review some tips for leading productive discussions, please turn to Appendix B at the end of this Leader's Guide.

The group participants will be provided an opportunity to apply what they've learned in Lessons 2–11. As the group leader, you can choose whether it would be appropriate for the group to discuss these assignments during this 10-minute time-slot.

DVD VIEWING (30 MINUTES)[1]

Play the session for *Why We Believe the Bible* that corresponds to the lesson you're studying. You may choose to pause the DVD at crucial points to check for understanding and provide clarification. Or, you may choose to watch the DVD without interruption.

DISCUSSION AND CLOSING (20 MINUTES)

Foster discussion on what was taught during John Piper's session. You may do this by first reviewing the DVD notes (under the heading "While You Watch the DVD, Take Notes") and then proceeding to the discussion questions, listed under the heading "After You Watch the DVD, Discuss What You've Learned." These discussion questions are meant to be springboards that launch the group into further and deeper discussion. Don't feel constrained to cover these questions if the group discussion begins to move in other helpful directions.

Close the time by briefly reviewing the application section and the homework that is expected for the next lesson. Pray and dismiss.

BEFORE LESSON 12

It is important that you encourage the group participants to complete the preparatory work for Lesson 12. This assignment invites the participants to reflect on what they've learned and what remaining questions they still have. As the group leader, this would be a helpful assignment for you to complete as well. In addition, you may want to write down the key concepts of this DVD series that you want the group participants to walk away with.

DURING LESSON 12

The group participants are expected to complete a reflection exercise as part of their preparation for Lesson 12. The bulk of the group time during this last lesson should be focused on reviewing and synthesizing what was learned. Encourage each participant to share some recorded thoughts. Attempt to answer any remaining questions that they might have.

To close this last lesson, you might want to spend extended time in prayer. If appropriate, take prayer requests relating to what the participants have learned in these twelve weeks, and bring these requests to God.

It would be completely appropriate for you, the group leader, to give a final charge or word of exhortation to end this group study. Speak from your heart and out of the overflow of joy that you have in God.

Please receive our blessing for all of you group leaders who choose to use this study guide:

> *The* LORD *bless you and keep you; the* LORD *make his face to shine upon you and be gracious to you; the* LORD *lift up his countenance upon you and give you peace. (Numbers 6:24–26)*

NOTES

1. Thirty minutes is only an approximation. Some of the sessions are shorter; some are longer. You may need to budget your group time differently, depending upon which session you are viewing.

APPENDIX A
SIX-SESSION INTENSIVE OPTION

WE UNDERSTAND THAT THERE ARE circumstances which may prohibit a group from devoting twelve sessions to this study. In view of this, we have designed a six-session intensive option for groups that need to complete the material in less time. In the intensive option, the group should meet for two hours each week. Here is our suggestion for how to complete the material in six weeks:

Week 1 Introduction to the Study Guide and Lesson 1
Week 2 Lessons 2 and 3 (DVD Sessions 1 and 2)
Week 3 Lessons 4 and 5 (DVD Sessions 3 and 4)
Week 4 Lessons 6 and 7 (DVD Sessions 5 and 6)
Week 5 Lessons 8 and 9 (DVD Sessions 7 and 8)
Week 6 Lessons 10 and 11 (DVD Sessions 9 and 10)

Notice that we have not included Lesson 12 in the intensive option. Moreover, because each participant is required to complete two lessons per week, it will be necessary to combine the number of "days" within each lesson so that all of the material is covered. Thus, for example, during Week 2 in the intensive option, each participant will complete

- Lesson 2, Days 1 and 2, on the first day;
- Lesson 2, Days 3 and 4, on the second day;

› Lesson 2, Day 5 and Lesson 3, Day 1, on the third day;
› Lesson 3, Days 2 and 3, on the fourth day;
› Lesson 3, Days 4 and 5, on the fifth day.

Because of the amount of material, we recommend that students focus on questions marked with an asterisk (*) first, and then, if time permits, complete the rest of the questions.

APPENDIX B

LEADING PRODUCTIVE DISCUSSIONS

Note: This material has been adapted from curricula produced by The Bethlehem Institute (TBI), a ministry of Bethlehem Baptist Church. It is used by permission.

IT IS OUR CONVICTION THAT the best group leaders foster an environment in their group that engages the participants. Most people learn by solving problems or by working through things that provoke curiosity or concern. Therefore, we discourage you from ever "lecturing" for the entire lesson. Although a group leader will constantly shape conversation, clarifying and correcting as needed, they will probably not talk for the majority of the lesson. This study guide is meant to facilitate an investigation into biblical truth—an investigation that is shared by the group leader and the participants. Therefore, we encourage you to adopt the posture of a "fellow-learner" who invites participation from everyone in the group.

It might surprise you how eager people can be to share what they have learned in preparing for each lesson. Therefore, you should invite participation by asking your group participants to share their discoveries. Here are some of our "tips" on facilitating discussion that is engaging and helpful:

› Don't be uncomfortable with silence initially. Once the first participant shares their response, others will be likely to join in. But if you cut the silence short by prompting them, then they are more likely to wait for you to prompt them every time.

- Affirm every answer, if possible, and draw out the participants by asking for clarification. Your aim is to make them feel comfortable sharing their ideas and learning, so be extremely hesitant to "shut down" a group member's contribution or "trump" it with your own. This does not mean, however, that you shouldn't correct false ideas—just do it in a spirit of gentleness and love.
- Don't allow a single person, or group of persons, to dominate the discussion. Involve everyone, if possible, and intentionally invite participation from those who are more reserved or hesitant.
- Labor to show the significance of their study. Emphasize the things that the participants could not have learned without doing the homework.
- Avoid talking too much. The group leader should not monopolize the discussion, but rather guide and shape it. If the group leader does the majority of the talking, the participants will be less likely to interact and engage, and therefore they will not learn as much. Avoid constantly adding the "definitive last word."
- The group leader should feel the freedom to linger on a topic or question if the group demonstrates interest. The group leader should also pursue digressions that are helpful and relevant. There is a balance to this, however: the group leader *should* attempt to cover the material. So avoid the extreme of constantly wandering off topic, but also avoid the extreme of limiting the conversation in a way that squelches curiosity or learning.
- The group leader's passion, or lack of it, is infectious. Therefore, if you demonstrate little enthusiasm for the material, it is almost inevitable that your participants will likewise be bored. But if you have a genuine excite-

ment for what you are studying, and if you truly think Bible study is worthwhile, then your group will be impacted positively. Therefore, it is our recommendation that before you come to the group, you spend enough time working through the homework and praying, so that you can overflow with genuine enthusiasm for the Bible and for God in your group. This point cannot be stressed enough. Delight yourself in God and in his Word!

desiringGod

If you would like to further explore the vision of God and life presented in this book, we at Desiring God would love to serve you. We have hundreds of resources to help you grow in your passion for Jesus Christ and help you spread that passion to others. At our website, desiringGod.org, you'll find almost everything John Piper has written and preached, including more than thirty books. We've made over twenty-five years of his sermons available free online for you to read, listen to, download, and in some cases watch.

In addition, you can access hundreds of articles, listen to our daily internet radio program, find out where John Piper is speaking, learn about our conferences, discover our God-centered children's curricula, and browse our online store. John Piper receives no royalties from the books he writes and no compensation from Desiring God. The funds are all reinvested into our gospel-spreading efforts. DG also has a whatever-you-can-afford policy, designed for individuals with limited discretionary funds. If you'd like more information about this policy, please contact us at the address or phone number below. We exist to help you treasure Jesus Christ and his gospel above all things because he is most glorified in you when you are most satisfied in him. Let us know how we can serve you!

Desiring God
Post Office Box 2901
Minneapolis, Minnesota 55402

888.346.4700
mail@desiringGod.org
www.desiringGod.org

Personal Notes

Personal Notes

Personal Notes

Personal Notes

Personal Notes

Personal Notes